Late Spring

A Life's Journey
Tung Lau

Annie Lau

First published in Great Britain in 2023

Published by Baa Baa Press
Email: Baabaapress@gmail.com

A CIP catalogue of this book is available from the British
Library

ISBN: 978-1-7393230-0-4

For my Parents

Contents

Preface

A Daughter's Thoughts

The traumas and pain of my mother's life were by no means unusual for a woman of her generation, being born into a life whose rhythms and values had not seen change for generations; a life where poverty and suffering was commonplace and the life of a girl considered of no importance compared to that of a boy. Yet despite the hardships she endured her journey was not one of sadness or misery, but one of transformative joy.

China in the 1930s was a vast nation convulsing with change. After 2,000 years of imperial rule, the unimaginable had happened; the Qing dynasty had been overthrown in 1912 and China was now ruled, not by an emperor, but by a Republic: the Nationalist Party, led first by Sun Yat Sen and then Chiang Kai Shek.

My mother was born in a small town which sat on a peninsula jutting into the South China Sea in the province of Guangdong. There had been an ongoing power struggle between the Nationalists, who had taken power in 1911, and the Communist party since the 1920s. Banditry and lawlessness, rebellions and attempted coups, these had been rife since the turn of the century, but none of these, often harrowing events, touched my mother for the first seven years or so of her life. Not even when civil war officially erupted between the Nationalists and the Communists in 1931, the year she was born, ensconced as they were within a small provincial town, surrounded on three sides by the sea, in the far south of China. Instead, it was the Japanese invasion of southern China in 1938 that catapulted her into poverty and a near lifetime of struggle.

The Japanese invasion touched everyone. Even today, many Chinese of my mother's generation cannot forgive or forget the savagery and brutality they both witnessed and endured. Yet, for my mother, even though she never fully recovered from the losses she experienced as a girl, it was her encounter with Jesus that was to become the defining moment of her life. Because of healing that came through being embraced by love and acceptance, she was able to choose to live, not in regret and despair, but joy and forgiveness, both of which were driven by an unquenchable spiritual thirst to know and love God.

It is this desire and thirst for love and joy that has made the strongest impression on me. A lasting gift to a daughter who would often challenge her opinions and views, a trait not seen as becoming in a traditional Chinese family. But perhaps my rebellious questioning mirrored her own, far stronger, inner rebellious spirit. A spirit that allowed her to stubbornly persist in situations that seemed hopeless and fuel a sheer strength of will that refused to accept seemingly inevitable courses of action when she believed them to be wrong.

I am aware of course that this biography of my mother leans heavily on my own reflections, beliefs and memories. She shared her life story with myself and my siblings as often as we would allow. Like all children, when young, I listened with eagerness and then impatience as my mother spoke of stories from her life that I deemed repetitive. When older, I became more aware of the emotional trauma she had experienced but became less interested in listening as I believed, wrongly of course, that I had heard all her stories before and knew as much as I needed. Thankfully, her church, as part of their project to share testimonies of their members, recorded, by audio, many of her recollections and I am grateful to them; both for their initiative in recording my mother and then allowing me access to their original, unedited material.

Many other pieces of information such as names and, especially dates, have been supplied by various members of my family, but the focus is not the chronological accuracy of my mother's life; my intention is not to create a listing of precise incidents. It is impossible to now give wholly watertight accurate details of a world that has now passed. Instead, my hope in writing this story is twofold: that readers find benefit to their own spiritual journeys through my mother's experiences and that my mother can, at last, be given a voice, a chance to be heard. For most of her life she had been unable to choose, to speak, to express opinions without the weight of the demands of the responsibilities of a daughter, mother and wife. It is impossible to imagine what she might have achieved had she been free to choose. Her life was bound by her circumstances which shaped her. It was only in her identity as a child of God: loved, valued and protected, that she was able to partly glimpse the unbroken, beautiful person God saw her to be.

Most of the stories in this book are focused on my mother's own experiences but many involve the action of third parties. My focus is on her perspective, but I am also aware that decisions made by my mother, which she considered right, can be seen differently by others who experienced the same event. The accuracy of events can also be disputed. She often expressed the pain of having been misunderstood and it is unlikely that those who disagreed with her decisions when she made them will feel differently now if they are gracious enough to read this book.

None of us are perfect. We are flawed human beings, made in the image of the perfect God, yet ourselves still imperfect.

Truly, only in God can we trust.

Annie
Liverpool, May 2022

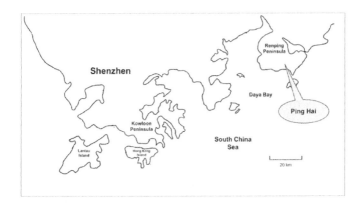

Chapter 1

A Promise of Spring

My mother was born during a winter's solstice in 1931, in a small town in southern China, located on what is now known as the Renping Peninsula, a small projection of land surrounded on three sides by the South China Sea; a small segment of a vast country; 79 km from Hong Kong, 2,168 km distant from Beijing, and 9,673 km from the United Kingdom. In view of the circumstances and timing of her arrival, her family named her, somewhat appropriately, if rather unimaginatively, 'Tung', the Chinese word for 'winter'. It was a birth date that she shared with both her brother and mother; a coincidence that I used to believe had to have been contrived for convenience in a society where birthdates of children were of less importance than they are today, but now, I can see that it was not so improbable after all; a change of perspective that has come with a greater acceptance of life that is never painted in thick lines segregating one primary incident from another but as a palette where events, decisions, people are a blurred synthesis of all that we are.

The beginnings of who my mother was began in Ping Hai, an ancient town with roots dating back to the 14th century. At the time of my mother's birth, it was a prosperous, bustling town that served as a sea facing trading point for villages in its surrounding locality. The town itself was historically confined by ancient fortifications in the form of a stone wall but life and commerce would have long spilt beyond such confines. My mother was the eldest daughter of a modestly well to do trading family. She recalled how they would store goods for those that had come into the town for market days but had not sold all their wares.

It was an act that was demonstrative of her grandparents' kindnesses. Her grandmother was a large woman who would hide steamed buns in the sleeve of her voluminous outer clothing and hand them to the beggars who came to their door whilst her grandfather, a smaller, but kindly man, was given the nickname of 'Buddha' in recognition of his generosity to those around him.

In addition to the house, the family also owned three fishing vessels. My mother recalled going with her grandfather to the jetty to meet the fishing boats as they returned with their catch and how, on one particular night, she was taken out on one of the boats to go fishing with her grandfather. There, she lay on her back, rocked gently by the waves and stared up at the night sky. It remained with her as a moment of pure bliss; a moment surrounded by love and peace, when the world was full of possibilities and hope.

Such memories were indicative of the love she experienced as a girl. In a society where sons are still valued above daughters, my mother's childhood was unusual in that she was cherished and loved, irrespective of her gender. By the age of three, her dowry had already been set aside and although she had a younger brother, she was the favourite grandchild. The family traded in all kinds of goods but especially fish which they also caught and sold. Her love of seafood, especially fish, remained an ingrained passion throughout her life. In later years, she would recall vividly the taste of the sea urchins eaten lifted straight from the sea and how, as a favoured grandchild, she would be given the tastiest parts of any choice catch. Even at the dinner table, her love of fried fish skin meant older members would carefully remove the skin to give to her before the meal would begin. It was the only period in her life, until she met with Jesus, when she felt fully safe and fully loved.

Memories of her father are limited to only those first ten years of her life. He was the first son in three generations of his family and as such, all was done to safeguard his future happiness. To ensure an appropriate bride would be ready and waiting, a girl had been adopted as a very young child and raised within the family in preparation for future marriage. It was not an unusual arrangement and, until the loss of the family's fortunes and the death of her husband, my grandmother lived a life of leisure and ease. The family business was prosperous, and her in-laws capable and kind which meant she was able to spend her time shopping, dressmaking and attending local entertainments.

In the mid 1930s, movie theatres were gaining popularity in China but only in large, cosmopolitan cities such as Shanghai and Beijing. On the provincial Renping peninsula and ancient town of Hai Ping where my mother lived, movie theatres were probably as accessible as life size models of the moon and just as in demand. Instead, popular local entertainment took the form of Chinese opera, performed in pop-up open air theatres. These can still be found today around China and in Hong Kong during annual festivals. Unlike hushed auditoriums in western opera, these were and remain, loud, even raucous events, at least before the start of performances. There was no ticketing system. Anyone who wished to grab the best seats would have to arrive early and stake a spot by the placement of a wooden stool on which they would then have to sit to preserve their claim. My grandmother was prosperous enough to pay for a 'sitter' whose sole job was to literally keep a seat warm and attended to until she arrived to take her place. In view of such a life of ease, it is little wonder that my grandmother so lacked wisdom in dealing with life's vicissitudes when she later found herself a young widow with two small children under the age of ten.

Early Mishaps

Throughout her life, my mother had to bear with a number of physical ailments. The first, and most unusual, came about from an encounter with an angry wild pig when she was three years old. Even today, in China, it is common to see wild boar, not only in the countryside, but scavenging in heavily urbanised areas. Hong Kong, one of the most urbanised places on the planet, has frequent sightings of feral pigs. In 2020, office workers at the Bank of China tower in the Central district of Hong Kong, (a location akin to the City of London or Wall Street in New York) were both shocked and amused to find a family of wild hogs had converted the water feature in the forecourt of the bank into a boar bath. Both male and females have ferociously sharp tusks and can be very aggressive if provoked.

When three years old, my mother found herself on the sharp end of an argument with an enraged wild sow. While playing by some stone steps with another little girl, she was bitten on her left leg. In defence of the pig, my mother always argued that the sow had been afraid for her piglets; a sentiment that, as a mother later in life, she fully appreciated. The gash however was deep enough to show bone and for some days, my mother was feverish and ill. Today, it is likely that she would have required stitches and antibiotics but such medication in Ping Hai was unknown or unavailable. The wound was eventually healed by the use of a poultice made from mulberry leaves and other wild herbs found near the sea. She was left with a scar the length of her shin on the side of her calf.

We would probably never have been told of this incident had it not been for the strange lumpy scarring that remained. The bite had left a bacterium that would stay with her throughout her life. The lump was like an alien growth. It would thicken or subside without warning, but mostly, it would redden in bumps and bulges and cause untold itching and irritation. She was often an inpatient at hospitals for various ailments and remembered with pride how consultants would poke at her leg and show junior doctors the strange undiagnosed infection. With slaverings of steroids and innumerable Chinese herbs, the angry, lumpy growth did eventually shrink to near invisibility by the time she was in her 80s but I like to think, that if a biopsy could be taken today and a previously unknown bacteria discovered, she would have been tickled pink by the idea that she had contributed to the expansion of medical knowledge.

The incident with the wild boar had been potentially fatal but there were other, less dangerous, but equally impressively unusual events. Wild boar were commonplace, but equally so were cows, or bullocks as they were prevalent not for their meat, but for their labour. One method of dealing with a tooth abscess was to soak a rag in warm cow's urine. The unfortunate owner of the abscess would then bite on the urine-soaked rag and in this way, the infection was killed. A similar method was used when my mother had a boil on her right knee that did not heal. A poultice was again applied, but this time, cow dung was used. The knee healed but, as with her leg, it remained susceptible to rheumatism and inflammation throughout her life and needed an operation when she had settled in the UK.

All of these events were memorable, and they would probably have remained as the most memorable stories in an otherwise happy, uneventful childhood but instead, they became relegated to matters of minor, unusual interest only; that was because her world, and that of millions of others, changed forever with the onset of the 2nd Sino-Japanese war.

Chapter 2

An Empty House

There were three defining events in my mother's life: the deaths of her grandparents and father, marriage and her first encounter with God. Each of these events brought momentous changes to her life. Change, of course, is not necessarily negative. It is a fact of life. Without change, there is stagnation and with stagnation there is death but in my mother's case, the first of these changes brought nothing but disaster and trauma. She was not yet seven years old when the 2nd Sino-Japanese war broke out.

In the west, history of the first half of the 20th century is dominated by the events of two World Wars, bringing to mind battles in Europe and, to a lesser degree, conflict in the Pacific between allied forces and Japanese troops. The part Japan played in conflicts during this period is usually recognised only as it relates to engagement with western powers, but in the far east, a see-saw of territorial, political and cultural power struggles had been ongoing for centuries between China and its near neighbour, Japan. Historically, China had been the more powerful entity, but by the end of the 19th century, Japan's openness to modernisation and reform, especially of its armed forces, had coincided with the final death throes of China's last imperial rulers, the Qing dynasty. Simmering tensions resulted in the 1st Sino-Japanese war of 1894 to 1895. What became known as the 2nd Sino-Japanese war erupted in 1937 and ended in 1945, intersecting with the 2nd World War.

War with Japan was a brutal interlude to the existing tussle for power between Nationalists and Communists that had arisen from the tottering collapse of imperial rule. Official Chinese figures released in the China Daily in 2015 put the total figure of Chinese casualties, military and non-military, at thirty-five million. A more conservative figure, but no less staggering, was that of fifteen million deaths, estimated by a group at the University of Oxford which undertook research funded by the Leverhulme Trust in 2007. The war consumed the whole of China. Massacres and atrocities were common, the most infamous being the six-week rampage of rape, murder and wanton destruction committed by Japanese forces on the city of Nanjing (the then Nationalist capital of China). The southern province of Guangdong was over 1,400 kilometres from Nanjing, but it did not take long for the entire country to be overrun by Japanese forces who arrived in Guangdong in 1938.

It must have been terrifying for anyone, not least a young girl, to have lived through that moment in history. Whenever I asked her of her memories of that time, her replies were always in quiet, suppressed tones. She recalled the sound of the hobnailed boots as the Japanese soldiers marched, echoing probably the terror in her chest. More than eighty years later, I would still be able to sense the shudder that the memory of that sound evoked. The Sino-Japanese war is a long, well documented, catalogue of rape and murder: as a child as young as seven, she and the other women would rub their faces with dirt and soot to avoid unwanted attention from soldiers. On one occasion when they, and others, were running away from opposing forces and hiding in bushes, soldiers jabbed their long bayonets into the bushes indiscriminately, looking for anyone hidden in the foliage. To avoid the whole group being discovered, crying babies were smothered by their own mothers.

Perhaps the soldiers were as famished as the people they were killing. The same bayonets used to kill pregnant women and hidden civilians they would then use as cooking implements by impaling chickens alive and whole, roasting them, unplucked, over open fires. It was a time of famine and hardship. Living near to the sea, she, and others, would forage for kelp or other foods but starvation was never far away.

Within my own family, a child was born during this time. Feeding the mouths they had was already a challenge beyond their strength; my great grandmother took the newborn out of the house. When she returned, she returned alone. Tragedies like this were commonplace and it is unsurprising that, whether from disease, malnutrition or a combination of factors, my mother's small family was to see more fatalities. The war officially ended on the 2nd of September 1945 when the official surrender was signed by Emperor Hirohito onboard the USS Missouri. My mother was by then 9 years old but there would be no happy ending. Within a year and a half, her small, close-knit family was to be decimated. The first to die in her extended family had been an aunt, just before the end of the war. Three weeks later, her grandmother died, followed, a few months later, by her father and a year later, her grandfather.

One of the final memories she had of her father was that of kindness and love. She remembered him propped up in bed and then motioning her to take the small candy that was always given to patients after drinking bitter, Chinese herbal medicine. The medicines did not work. With the subsequent death of her elderly father-in-law, her mother was now left as a young widow with two small children. Life in 1930s China was harsh for women at the best of times. Now, after decades of social upheaval, a young woman with few skills, not even as a farmer, was thrown into a hungry void. It was not long before most of their possessions were sold. No doubt the sale of belongings had in all probability begun long before the death of her grandfather. Years of conflict, ill health and the social upheaval had left not just their family in dire straits, but all of Chinese society.

They had one remaining relative; a surviving aunt and it was to this aunt that they sometimes went for food. Even then, fragments of love surrounded her. At one meal, a dish consisted of meat cooked with a vegetable she did not like. She had to be coaxed to eat. Meat was incredibly scarce but instead of scolding her, her aunt placed a piece of pork in her mouth and told her to suck on the morsel until the taste of the unpleasant vegetable faded.

Such kindness in a sea of overwhelming confusion and sorrow could not last. Her aunt had married and in Chinese culture, a daughter once married is no longer part of her parents' family; she now belonged to her husband's family and her allegiances and thus resources had to be apportioned accordingly. They could not rely on her aunt and the sale of possessions would not be enough, especially when my grandmother's vulnerability and inexperience meant most of the family's belongings had been seized by unscrupulous neighbours or stolen by strangers. As a result, her mother would often be absent, sometimes for up to three days at a time, walking to different villages, looking for work as a labourer; she would carry loads or cut grass. Her brother, three years younger than herself, would be taken along, leaving my mother alone in an empty house, tasked with keeping out robbers and burning incense before the family altar on which she would place wine and slippers for those that had departed. Incredulously to our modern ears, she was left alone for a few days in the empty house with the body of her grandfather before he was buried. It is no wonder that the house, previously a locus of love and security, now became a place of fear and vulnerability.

Devoid of almost all belongings and furnishings, the dwelling was now cold, damp and dark. It was common for the house to be frequently flooded. Flood waters would race through the long corridor that ran the length of the house, bringing hordes of sea snakes that would writhe and wriggle in a demented dance as they were swept careeringly along. To escape both the flood waters and the seething, sinuous mass she would climb up the sides of the wall, looking for any foothold, and wait for the frenzy to abate.

When my siblings and I were children, we learnt to switch channels on the television whenever images of snakes or even worms appeared. Even material or images that resembled snake skins would cause my mother deep paranoia. Only when I grew older and listened with a more discerning ear to her stories of her childhood did I realise where her phobia came from. In later life she was eventually able to look on anything slightly reptilian without shrinking, a cause for celebration as it reflected the inner healing that had been ongoing in her life.

But all that was to come. The family home was now a place of shadows and ghosts. Feeling abandoned and unloved she would spend nights shivering, not with cold but with fear, as she waited for the dawn. A large kitchen knife would be placed across the bolts of the door, jammed in place by a rod of bamboo and a blanket would then be pulled up over her head; she did not dare lift her head from under the covers until she heard the morning birdsong and saw slivers of sunlight cut through the cracks in the wooden window slats. In truth, by then there was nothing left to steal but despite the terror that she felt, she was clear minded enough to do what she could to be safe. Determination and persistence through adversity that was to be a hallmark of her life was already apparent.

Traditionally, food in Chinese homes was cooked over a large stove built of stone or brick. The stove had an opening into which firewood was placed and on top, there would be a large opening over which a wok was set. Single person meals in 1930s China were an unknown concept. Families were large and, unless you were a beggar, lives were lived within extended households. The woks were large, heavy and inset into the stove with their rounded bottoms and could be as wide as 60 inches in diameter. These woks were not normally lifted from the stove as they were used for steaming, stewing as well as frying. When she was left alone in the house, the only food to be cooked was rice and salted egg. It clearly made little sense for a small child, hardly tall enough to reach the top of the stove, to cook such limited fare. The small bowl of rice and egg was taken to a neighbour who would cook it with her own family's meal. Although the neighbour was kind and pressed my mother to join them in eating the food the family was sharing, my mother was mortified and covered with a sense of shame at her own impoverishment.

Near Misses

Whenever my grandmother returned, my mother would rush to meet her. On one such occasion, she was caught in a storm in a flooded field. The whole event had a dreamlike quality. The waters rose to her chest and she would have drowned had not a stranger reached out with a hand and pulled her out. When she was in her eighties, and in and out of hospital, her beloved GP said of her that she had 'more lives than a cat'. Little did he know that she had had multiple lives, all of them charmed, or perhaps we should rather say, guarded by her Heavenly Father. The proximity of water and typhoons were a recurring event in her early life and the near miss in the field was not the only time in China when her life was nearly snuffed out. While working in a field, she and others were caught in one of the many recurring typhoons that are a feature of this part of the world. Water rushed down a gulley, washing away all their baskets.

In future years, the sea would again, continue to try and swallow my mother but unlike her fear of snakes, she was never left with any negativity or trepidation towards water, not even after her shipwreck on her journey to Hong Kong, a fact evidenced by the joy she discovered in the local swimming pool where she would spend hours immersed in tepid, chlorinated water, stopping her visits only when she could no longer manage to move more than a few feet unassisted on her Zimmer frame.

Life as a child and as an adult was a constant struggle but not without its moments of wonder. When still a child, she remembered the sense of absolute stillness when walking home over a mountain path. The silence was broken intermittently by the occasional chirp of birds and the sound of wildlife scampering through the undergrowth and then, the shock of coming face to face with a tiger. Perhaps it was more shocked than my mother, but we are thankful that the tiger was not hungry and my mother lived to tell the tale.

Bandits and Fights

Eventually, life became untenable in their hometown and the small family of three moved to another village where my grandmother found protection and a degree of security as the 2nd wife (or more likely, in view of the social conditions of the time, a concubine) of the village headman. It was in keeping with my mother's eventful history that he was also a local bandit. It may have been my mother's feistiness but the headman-cum-bandit took a liking to this combative small girl and while he was alive, they were safe from starvation and predation, but physical safety did not guard against emotional wounds. Local children would taunt my mother and her brother, calling them pieces of garbage and floating flotsam. True to her unwillingness to back down from any fight, she would give back taunts as good as she got but the barbs hit home.

Although she had shelter and food, she, her mother and brother were never fully accepted into this new community. When other children celebrated Chinese New Year with the traditional set of new clothes and ate within the warmth of a loving family, she sat outside, enviously listening to the sounds of laughter and joy of other children, feeling abandoned and ostracised for having no father and no true home.

Unfortunately, whatever protection and stability their new life brought them was not to last. In the same way she had witnessed her father and grandfather die whilst sitting bolt upright in their beds, her new foster father, who had at least treated her kindly, was also to meet his demise sitting bolt upright, dying slowly from bullet wounds sustained from a gun battle. She saw him carried into the house; dark stains from dried blood on his clothes and watched as his life slowly ebbed away over the course of many days. When he finally succumbed, the three of them were once again cast into the unknown.

Chapter 3

A Dangerous Journey

On the death of their erstwhile protector they found themselves again struggling to survive; hunting for anything edible along the beach that wrapped around their peninsula, sometimes stripping bark from trees in a vain attempt to fill their stomachs. It was an exhausting, wearying battle and so, when my mother was thirteen years old, my grandmother made the momentous decision to try their luck in Hong Kong. An acquaintance, known to my grandmother, had a son who worked in a hotel in the enclave and she suggested that mother and daughter take the journey with her when she went to join her son as there was greater possibility of making a living. Like all refugees and immigrants before and after, they took any connection, however slight, as an anchor upon which to latch their hopes.

Throughout the first few decades of the 20th century during the Chinese civil war and the subsequent Sino-Japanese war, Hong Kong had become a magnet for refugees: refugees from the Nationalists, refugees from the Communists and then refugees from the Japanese. Originally, the territory controlled by Britain comprised only the island itself, but it eventually expanded into the Kowloon peninsula and today, it extends even further into what is known as the New Territories; land that forms part of the Chinese province of Guangdong.

During the late 19th to early 20th century, movement and passage of people and goods from the mainland of China into Hong Kong and out again was frequent. For my mother, a journey to Hong Kong would be a dangerous one, to be taken by boat. By today's distances, travel to Hong Kong Island from the Renping peninsula is not an insurmountable distance. It lies approximately 80 kilometres, as the crow flies, to the southwest of my mother's hometown but, apart from the dangers of open water, the section of seas between Ping Hai and Hong Kong was renowned as pirate territory. Daya Bay, or Bias Bay as it was then known, is now most famous for being the location of a nuclear plant but in the early 20th century, it had been a hideout for pirates that plied across that section of the South China Sea, operating most prominently during the 1920s. Was the bandit who gave my mother a temporary home connected to the lawlessness of these men? In all likelihood, yes, but we shall never know for sure.

As to the route itself, maps of the coastline today from the town of Ping Hai on the Renping peninsula to Hong Kong shows that they would have had to cross Daya Bay, pass the large projection of landmass that is the Dapeng Peninsula, navigate through a section of Kowloon known as the Sai Kung Peninsula before they could reach the eastern coast of Hong Kong Island. In between, there are dotted islands of varying sizes; some habited, some not, but on even the smallest, it is not unusual for there to be a small temple or shrine to the gods of the sea. Common to all men and women who rely on the sea for their livelihood, superstitions run deep and insurance is sought against calamity by placating powerful deities in whose hands they believed their lives were kept.

With such dangers ahead, my grandmother decided to leave my uncle in the relative safety of their hometown. My mother, being a girl, was dispensable, but as the only son my uncle's life could not be risked. Selling the house and what land remained, the proceeds were given to a neighbour; the agreement being that my uncle would live with them until he came of age or the family could be reunited. It was not an arrangement my mother or her brother would have agreed with had they had a choice. Today, we are all too aware of the emotional needs of children and the toll that it can extract upon them as adults when such needs are not met, but when decisions are driven by questions of life or death, such considerations have to be regarded as dispensable niceties. Such was the predicament my grandmother found herself in when she resolved to leave for a city that must have sounded like a metropolis. My uncle, although he did not have to face the physical dangers and deprivations his sister encountered, would suffer all his life from the after effects of what he perceived as abandonment. Just as his sibling had to endure the shame of her loneliness and penury when she ate with her neighbour her solitary bowl of rice and salted egg and the taunts from other children, he too would, for the rest of his life, feel the burning humiliation of being treated as an inferior within the family he lived with; unloved and unvalued, without status and treated as a servant.

My uncle's relationship with my grandmother never fully recovered, feeling as he did that he had been rejected in favour of his sister. His feelings were exacerbated, when, years later, my grandmother remarried and had another son; a son of her old age whom she doted upon. This was yet to come, but then, little did he know that his own fate was predicated on being valued as a son, unlike that of his older sibling, who came within a hair's breadth of an even worse fate: being sold as slave labour. To be fair to my grandmother, her choices were limited. Starvation was an ever-present reality and it was only because she was advised that a daughter could be useful in a new life in Hong Kong that my mother escaped probable enslavement or worse and made the journey with her.

Although they shared only a few years together; those early years in their hometown and then for a few years in Hong Kong after my father paid a snakehead to smuggle him out of China, my mother's affection for her brother remained undiminished. Three years younger, he was more timid and diffident than his pugnacious older sister.

She would always laugh with affection when she recalled how they would hunt for sand crabs during those years of desperate hunger. My uncle would be too afraid of both dirt and skirmishes with other hungry foragers along the coastline, and would stand at a distance, waiting for his sister who would dive into the fray, digging into the wet sand, brawling and scraping with others to claim the prize of small crabs or other shellfish found on the shore.

By the end of the day, she would be covered from head to toe in mud and dirt, with only her eyes showing white, but triumphant with her catch, while my uncle would return home, still completely clean with not a spot of dirt or mud on his clothes. But such memories are few. Aged ten, my uncle remained in the relative safety of Ping Hai while his sister and mother journeyed on a small boat into tempestuous seas.

The boat that took my mother to Hong Kong carried five passengers and their belongings. All my mother and grandmother now had left, or could carry with them, was in the form of 2 large wicker baskets, one of which contained a large chinese quilt, which, unlike western quilts, was a blanket into which was sewn cotton or, if you were rich, silk wadding. The ones my mother carried with her on the small boat are long gone, but years later, when we emigrated to England, we also took with us large, padded quilts which we used for years when children. It has only been recently, when my sister unpicked these remaining quilts, that she found one filled with clumps of dense silk padding; material that has survived airborne travel, childhood traumas and damp trunks.

She never spoke of her thoughts or feelings when she stepped onboard the small wooden vessel that would take them to an unknown future. Perhaps life was too precarious already; death by starvation would be as final as death by drowning. Afterall, boats and the sea were not a mystery to her; she had played on them, slept on them and spent her happiest moments on them. Despite having already narrowly missed being drowned when caught in a typhoon in a flooded field she had no fear of water, but like so much of my mother's life, the journey was anything other than uneventful.

They were caught in a storm and to avoid sinking, threw as much as they could overboard but managed to save their two precious wicker baskets from being lost. Eventually, they found refuge on one of the many small islands that are dotted around this stretch of water. The island was uninhabited, but it had a small, broken-down temple in which they took shelter. There, they stayed for three days until the storm abated and they were able to resume their journey, refilling the boat with sand as ballast before they set sail.

They finally arrived in Hong Kong at night, landing on a beach that has since been erased by the territory's voracious demand for land along the waterfront. The once sizeable bay on the north-eastern shore of Hong Kong Island, previously known simply as Sai Wan, is now the site of identical lego like housing estates that have eaten up the sandy beaches that were previously home to a number of small villages before Hong Kong's inexorable expansion out from its shoreline.

Until the 1980s when the Mass Transit Rail opened a station there, it was still considered something of an outlier from the main central hub to its west. Perhaps as an echo of its previously rustic history, it retains some surprisingly green areas and has a less frenetic air to it than the busier western coast of the island. Even so, today, there is no moment, night or day, when lights signifying human activity cannot be seen reaching out from any point along the Hong Kong coastline, but in 1945, after days of hardship and exhaustion, they were greeted by a silent darkness; there were no lights beyond the beach at all as they landed.

They slept that first night, out in the open, on the streets. I like to think that my mother, though tired, was excited by the prospect of new discoveries and opportunities but in reality, I suspect that her overwhelming emotion was relief and exhaustion. Not for the first, nor would it be the last time, she had been transplanted from one life to another.

Inedible fish and Rotten Eggs

Hong Kong was, and is, a heaving entrepot of trade. Its 'fragrant' harbour gave it a perfect gateway into China and led to its colonisation in the 19th century by the British. However, despite its status as a British enclave and the presence of British and Commonwealth troops at the start of World War two, it was not saved from hostilities. Bombed by the Japanese, it was then bombed again by the United States navy until cessation of hostilities in 1945. Seeking sanctuary from the Japanese invasion of Guangdong province, in the three years from 1938 to 1941, swathes of mainland Chinese entered the territory, by most counts, over 750 000; an incomprehensible mass of humanity on the move. By 1941, the estimated population of Hong Kong stood at 1.6 million, nearly half a million of which were homeless.

When hostilities shifted to embrace this seemingly innocuous piece of land, the mobile, ever changing population again dispersed and by the end of the war, according to official Hong Kong figures, it had shrunk to a mere 600,000. But this small fragment of land has always been a nexus of shifting transients. Once armed conflict ended the city became again a place of opportunity and profit. Migrants, like my mother, once again surged in, repopulating the slums and generating labour for the rebuilding and creation of modern day Hong Kong. The 1961 census shows that the population had grown to 3,129,648. Today, it stands at nearly 7.5 million.

When my mother arrived, the population was smaller but much poorer. The day after their arrival, they shouldered their two baskets of belongings and walked to Shek Tong Tsui, on the north-western shoreline of the island, where the old lady's son worked and where they would have a place to stay. Maps of the period show it to have been part of the most densely built up area on Hong Kong Island at the time. By road today, the journey is approximately 13.5 kilometres, or eight miles. It is likely they took a similar route, following any main roads that curved along the coast and avoiding mountain paths that can still be explored today by ramblers seeking an escape from the city.

Staying long term with the old woman and her son was not an option and after leaving their initial temporary lodgings, they moved from place to place. At one stage, both mother and daughter lived in a lean to on Big Wave Beach (now a favourite spot with surfers or wave watchers) later finding a spot under a staircase in one of the many deserted, bombed out houses in Sai Wan Ho, a busy district on the north-eastern shore of Hong Kong. They cut grass, used for feeding pigs, and worked as labourers, carrying loads, filling in bomb craters and breaking stones for use in construction. Being small and nimble, my mother would also be able to earn money by running onto bombed out sites and stealing bricks which could be sold for a penny each. Desirable sites were much fought over and were often guarded by gangs or the police.

She had to be fast and fearless and was often successful but even so, for a time, food was even scarcer than in their hometown as they could no longer forage, even along the shoreline: there was too much competition and too many people. As a result, my mother's stomach became distended from malnutrition, a condition that we have now come to associate with starving children in parts of Africa. Grandmother was at a loss to understand why her daughter's stomach seemed so full when she had had nothing to eat; all the while my poor mother writhed in agony holding her aching belly. Neither of them understood then that it was due to a deficient diet and even if they had known, there would have been nothing they could have done to ease her pain.

Life was most definitely a struggle, but my mother's determination and sheer stubborn pig headedness was to prove invaluable in these difficult times. When they first arrived, they had to rely on other migrants for help and advice to obtain work. On the second morning of her arrival, she was to follow their acquaintance to a labouring site. The location was quite a distance away and they would have to take the tram, which continues to this day to provide a cheap method of transport from east to west of the main populated areas of north Hong Kong Island.

My grandmother was still half asleep when her daughter woke at daybreak to get ready. Rummaging in her pocket, my grandmother pulled out what she thought was enough money for her daughter's fare on the tram. By the time my mother arrived at the assigned meeting point there was already a disorganised crowd trying to find an opening on any approaching tram. Being small and wiry, she was able to scramble on but had to leave behind the woman who was supposed to be her guide. Undaunted, there was nothing to do but get to her destination and find work. There would be no difficulty in knowing where to alight as most of the people on the tram would be heading to the same location. However, it was only when she had squeezed on that she discovered she had only enough for a one-way journey. Her stubborn pride that was to be a feature throughout her life meant she was unwilling to borrow or ask for help; her only option at the end of the working day was to follow the tracks whence the way she came. Walking for hours on foot after a full day labouring, she returned exhausted and seething with anger, but she knew that it would be fruitless to tell her mother of her day's predicament and hardship. She ended the day with an angry, brusque, "I'm home!" before slamming the door behind her as the only way to vent her anger.

Eventually, they earned enough each day to rent a small room, but food was still a monotonous repetition of rice and dried radishes. Having lived her short life by the sea and as a child, fed on the choicest pieces of seafood, mother and daughter longed for the taste of fish. One vivid memory my mother would retell was of seeing some small fish being sold very cheaply at the end of the day while on her way home from work. She pounced on them and displayed them triumphantly to her mother. Both were wildly excited to be able to eat something other than the plain rice that was their daily fare, but their disappointment was acute when they realised that, in their excitement, they had forgotten to clean out the fish bile. On taking the first bite, they discovered the whole dish was inedible and had to be thrown away. It was with dismay that they had to return to their normal fare of plain rice and radishes.

Another powerful memory that remained sharply etched for my mother during this time was her experience of selling eggs. Initially, when directed by my grandmother of this plan, she refused. She knew that the job would subject her to verbal abuse, but her mother's response was equally firm: she decided an empty stomach would soon lessen her daughter's resistance and left my mother without any dinner until she acquiesced. Hungry and feeling unloved, she sat on the doorsteps of the house where they rented a room until the landlady took pity and gave her a bowl of day-old rice. Although she was stubborn and combative, her mother was the only person she had left. Continued refusal was not an option and so, aggrieved but powerless, she eventually capitulated.

To sell eggs, one has to first buy eggs. This was done via the market in Sai Wan Ho where they lived at the time. Eggs were sold but only in large trays but my mother had enough money only for half a tray. Small and wafer thin, she found it difficult to be noticed or taken seriously. Undaunted, she pestered strangers until she found someone willing to share the cost of a full tray which they then divided between them. Successful in her first stage of her new egg selling venture, she then had to find buyers. This was done by placing her wares on a smaller tray, which she then strapped from her neck and shoulders, similar to the method used by ushers back in the days when one could buy ice-creams during intermissions at the cinema in Britain; something that was still common in my own childhood. She would then walk the local streets, crying out that eggs were for sale. Then, as now, dwellings would be multi-storied above shops. Customers would save themselves the effort of running down to street level and shout down from their windows. If they were interested, they would lower a bag with their money, together with a bowl into which eggs would be placed and then hauled back up through the open window.

To ensure they were buying only the freshest of goods, they would want assurance the eggs they were buying were not rotten. To do this, my mother would select an egg she knew to be fresh, break it open into the proffered bowl as proof. Since eggs were bought and eaten on the day, no one objected to buying an egg that had already been cracked open, so long as they had seen it being done. If the customers were happy with the sample egg, she would include, with the batch sold, one or two that were not so fresh.

Inevitably, when she walked the same round the next day she would be pulled up for her tricks and receive a round of verbal abuse, and, if she were not quick enough to escape, a few physical blows as well. My mother was not an unfeeling automaton and the abuse thrown at her cut deep but what could she do. Her only choice was to stay silent and take her punishment.

Any eggs not sold would be carefully stored at night. In the heat of subtropical Hong Kong, with no refrigeration, eggs would be hung from the ceiling to take advantage of any breeze and to keep them safe from rats. Such efforts were not always successful. On more than one occasion she would be woken by eggs exploding from the heat in the middle of the night.

Making a living was hard. She was a hawker, selling merchandise without a licence and just as she was chased by police when she scoured bricks from bombed out sites, now too, she also had to watch out for policemen. If caught, they would face a $5 dollar fine, an insurmountable sum for someone like my mother, but more importantly, their goods would be confiscated.

To the many street sellers, policemen were without pity and the bane of their lives. On a number of occasions she was nearly caught. She often told how, being small, and rather nippy, she ran as fast as she could towards the sea, away from the built-up buildings facing inland, with her long pigtails flailing behind her. One policeman was fitter than most and grabbed hold of her clothing, but my mother wriggled and struggled for dear life, managing to free herself at the cost of a torn tunic.

All these experiences meant the tenacious young girl grew into a combative teenager, ever ready to engage in verbal fights, never happy until her opponents cried with shame. I would not have recognised this skinny, loud, mouthy girl had I met her all those years ago, so different was she to the measured, joyful woman she later became. But we are moulded by our circumstances and even as the choppy waters she encountered at the start of her journey to Hong Kong settled into calmer circumstances, her life would soon be upturned yet again.

Chapter 4

Marketable Bride

By the time she was seventeen, my mother had been in Hong Kong for four years, by which time she had found a stable job in a shoe making factory and no longer needed to scrape around for broken bricks or run from overzealous police. She was still painfully thin but had stretched upwards and was taller than average for a southern Chinese girl. It was this attribute that decided my father's mind when looking for a bride. As my mother would always tell us, he wanted to ensure that his children would not be short, like 'hammered in nails'.

According to my father, he had seen my mother from afar and made enquiries. An older Shanghainese woman who lived in the same building as mother and daughter acted as matchmaker. When she enquired of my grandmother whether her daughter was available for marriage the response was without surprises; "What else are daughters for?" Thus, it was that my mother came home one day to find a strange man in their living quarters. Nothing was said between them, not least because he spoke with a northern dialect which she could not understand. Confused, she kept her head down and focused on eating her rice into which she would occasionally dip some shrimp paste from the tip of her chopsticks. It was not until he had left that she was informed that a marriage had been arranged. Her initial refusal was met with a slap to her face. She was told that an agreement had been reached in which my father would pay my grandmother HK$300 to marry her daughter. In addition, he would look after, not only his future wife, but his mother-in-law, in life and in death. In other words, he would support my grandmother financially until her death then ensure she was given a proper burial. In effect, my mother had been sold.

Decades later, even after she had come to love my father deeply, this event would still rouse profound feelings of rejection and loss of self-worth. In her eyes, her own mother had sold her 'like a piglet'. At the time, she believed that she had no need of a husband. She now had a stable job and could provide food and shelter for herself and her remaining parent, but a life of independence was no longer open to her; choices had been made on her behalf. Today, we wonder why a girl of my mother's spirit would accept such a fate, but she was a girl whose only close emotional bond was with her mother; a mother whom she both loved and hated with equal ferocity; a girl now becoming a woman, desperate for love and acceptance. In any event, despite four years in Hong Kong, she knew no-one else. Refusal was not an option.

She met my father again only once before they were married, if 'met' is the word that can be used. They had arranged to meet at a cinema. Tickets had been purchased by my father in advance and one given to his prospective bride before the show. She arrived and sat in her prescribed seat. The cinema was dark, and she was too nervous and shy to look either left or right to check whether her intended groom was in the seat next to her. She never did find out if he was there. Years later, when asked, he would only smile, enjoying his secret joke but I am pretty sure that he was there, holding in his laughter.

A Shandong Man

To understand the rest of my mother's life, it is necessary to know a little about my father. Named Lau Yuk Shan, he was the eldest son of a large extended family in the north-eastern province of Shandong. His father worked as a clerk in a nearby town, but his grandfather had owned a thriving wooden furniture business which, unfortunately, had been inadvertently burnt down when an uncle played with matches in the courtyard of the storage area. My father was a large man, with an even larger personality and explosive temper; a born risk taker and adventurer, he was willing to try his hand at almost anything. His approach to life was always that bigger was better, whether it was wallpaper patterns, size of furniture or food portions. Being cautious was not in his vocabulary but neither was he stingy or mean. If he had had a motto I like to think that it would have been, 'Nothing is impossible'. This approach to life's possibilities ranged from keeping adult geese in an urban back garden to knocking up a walk-in aviary behind my long suffering mother's kitchen, complete with tree sized branches from the local park, or walking home with half a cow over his shoulder from the meat market when taxi drivers, understandably, declined to take his fare.

My paternal grandfather had wanted his eldest son to either work in the fields or be apprenticed to a metal worker. Neither of these appealed to my father and at the age of fourteen, after a final argument, he threw down his hoe, climbed over the wall of his family home and left. He had absolutely nothing at all to call his own except the clothes on his back. On his way out of the village, a neighbour gave him the inner tube of his bicycle tyre for him to sell. My father remembered this neighbour and fifty years later when he returned to his village, he sought out the neighbour to thank him and return his gift with interest.

My father's home village was too small to contain his resourcefulness, enterprise and sheer energy. We know he went first to Yantai, the largest city nearest to his village, finding work as a delivery boy for restaurants and then, in the kitchens as an apprentice. The profession was made for him: food and its preparation and consumption became a passion which he lived and breathed and sometimes dreamed. My mother told me of how he would wake at night, sit bolt upright, and move his right hand in the motion of frying a wok, all whilst still asleep.

Travelling through China, he eventually found himself apprenticed in a large kitchen in Beijing where he stayed for a number of years. Traditional restaurant kitchens in China were large, supporting dozens, if not scores of men and boys, working in different stations, similar to the set-up of restaurants today, but on a much larger scale. There was no formal training and apprentices had to learn by watching, watching and waiting for opportunities. Occasionally, a master chef would take a shine to an apprentice and throw them some tidbits of advice or help but it was a dog-eat-dog world. Just as my mother had to fight and tussle for survival, my father too, had to be enterprising to succeed. Such drive and sheer determination can be illustrated by how he learnt to hand pull noodles.

In northern China, wheat is a more popular staple than rice and hand pulled noodles are a great favourite as the technique develops the gluten and, when done well, ensures a texture whereby the noodles are springy yet firm. Wanting to learn this skill, he collected blobs of unused dough from the end of each working day and for three nights running, he used the stub of a candle he had saved and practised what he had observed, not stopping till he finally felt he had mastered the technique.

The next time a customer asked for a bowl of hand pulled noodles, (every portion was made individually) my father sprang into action before anyone else could respond, producing the noodles, cooking them and presenting them to an astounded master chef. More importantly, the customer praised the cooking and sent his compliments to the kitchen. Years later when he had his own business and before hand pulling noodles became a familiar sight in the UK, he would often give a party piece to customers by 'pulling' long, thin strings of noodles from a block of dough. It was always a favourite with customers, and Dad, ever the showman, glowed with the sheer pleasure of entertaining as he would end his display with a flourish of noodles draped over his arm like an edible curtain.

Chapter 5

Marriage

My father was eleven years older than my mother and had arrived in Hong Kong in 1947. He found work as a chef in kitchens around the territory and by the standards of the day as a labourer, albeit a skilled one, earned a good wage, certainly good enough to marry and start a family and support a mother-in-law. Yet despite the money in his pocket and his undoubted skill and drive, his was but one wage in a growing family. That being the case, however generous my father was, he had not counted on having to support an additional family when my grandmother remarried and had a son.

My father was not a stingy man and was more than willing to help his mother-in-law and also my mother's brother in China for whom he arranged to bring down to Hong Kong via the use of a snakehead a few years after their marriage, but my grandmother's interpretation of their bargain was a cause of deep friction between husband and wife.

Matters were not helped by the fact that my new grandfather was never able, or perhaps willing, to find gainful employment. He was one of the many Nationalist soldiers who had found their way into Hong Kong at the end of the civil war. I have only a few memories of him: a neat, tidy man who had an obsession with cleanliness. I saw him once when he visited the UK in the 70s but by the time I made the journey to Hong Kong as an adult, he had already passed away.

As a result, my grandmother, and subsequently her new son, who was the same age as my eldest brother, spent most of her days with us while Dad was at work. My father was not adverse to mother and son eating three meals a day with us six days a week, but my grandmother was too avaricious or too foolish to appreciate any limits. To her, my father was an inexhaustible piggy bank; raided with impunity.

On one rare occasion when my father was home for a meal and not at work, he seethed with anger when he saw my grandmother pick out the choicest pieces of meat and give them to her own son, leaving pieces of fat for his own children. Rice, kerosene and cooking oil would also disappear at an alarming rate, or, as my mother would say, "They walked". Too scared to ask for additional money, my mother saved from her housekeeping to satisfy her mother's demands. My grandmother believed that she was taking only what was hers by right, as per their original agreement, but her behaviour was a cause of unspoken tension between my parents. My father was an old fashioned man with an explosive temper. He saw no need for my grandmother to remarry, especially when she now had a source of support; neither could he confront her directly as she was his mother-in-law, but her immoderate actions meant that he would often take out his frustrations on his wife. My poor mother often described herself as sandwich filling; caught between her fearsome husband and the constant unreasonable demands of her mother who, despite her simmering resentment, she still desperately looked to for love and affirmation.

Dark Days

Conflict and misery caused by my grandmother's unwise actions would follow my mother throughout most of her life. She had been angry at being sold in marriage and in the early years of her marriage, she resented being treated as an unpaid servant by my father. Although he softened as he grew older, Dad was a man who was clear in his views on the apportionment of responsibilities within a marriage: a wife's primary responsibilities were to take care of her husband and her children. Each night after work, however late, she was expected to wait up for him and prepare water for his bath and to wash his feet, drying meticulously between each toe with a towel. Her isolation and wretchedness was made worse by the fact that, initially, she could not understand a single word spoken by her new husband since his dialect was northern, nearer Mandarin and hers southern, more akin to Cantonese.

Years of struggle; a buried sense of abandonment from the loss of her father and grandparents and feelings of low self-worth led to darkness and despair that overwhelmed her; so much so that she attempted suicide by jumping from a bridge into a river only to be pulled out by a passing stranger. Bedraggled and wet she returned home to an unsympathetic husband who completely ignored her half-drowned state.

This period of her life was one of the lowest in a lifetime that was filled with hardships and sufferings. Unlike other stories from her past she shared this attempted suicide with me only once or twice, but she, as well as my siblings and I, are grateful that once again, a passing stranger saved her. Indeed, passing strangers feature in at least three major moments of her life. The first was when she was pulled from a flooded field in China, the second, when a stranger saved her from her suicide attempt and the third was to come many years later and thousands of miles distant, in the UK when she was desperately looking for a way to stay spiritually afloat.

Motherhood

My mother would always remain sandwiched in her loyalties between her mother and her husband, but despite initial dark days in her marriage, not all memories were bleak. Dad would take my mother to watch Chinese opera or the cinema. My father's work was physically hard and he would often escape for a nap in cemeteries, lying on top of stacked coffins to ensure that no one would find him. Chinese opera would often take place in the open air and he would avail himself of the opportunity for more sleep, but of course, only after downing a few bottles of beer he had bought with him. He was a man who lived his life in black and white with no room for compromise.

One time, when waiting in line for the cinema, a man jumped the queue in front of them. So incensed was my father that he physically lifted him off the ground with one hand, grabbing him by his tunic, and levered him from one spot to another, rather like a one-armed fork lift truck, before dropping him onto another, less occupied, spot.

Life progressed and children were born. Many years ago our family had an old, faded black and white photograph of my mother with my two eldest brothers. The photograph has since been lost, but it showed them standing on a hill, covered with spindly grey trees and vegetation. My brothers were no more than four and two, or perhaps even younger, I can no longer recall. But theirs were not the faces that drew me. Rather it was my mother's. I can still see before me her open face, smiling. Life was hard but life was life.

The background to the photograph reflects where they had lived when my two eldest brothers were born; in one of the many shanty towns and squatter huts that dotted the hillsides of Hong Kong Island at the time. But my eldest brother was not the eldest child. We have no photographic reminder of what she looked like, but we did have an older sister who died before my eldest brother was born. My mother never spoke of it. We managed only scraps of information from our grandmother who would always whisper when she spoke of our dead sister even when no one was near; it was a memory too painful to bear. But despite this loss, three healthy sons arrived, to be followed by three daughters.

After the birth of my second brother, they moved from the hillside to a stone hut in Hung Hom, on Kowloon. Here it was that my third brother and eldest sister were born. The hut was the size of a small single room, in front of which ran an open sewer past which human waste would routinely flow. It was a harsh existence and both of her children born here had traumatic beginnings.

My third brother had a breached birth, welcoming the world feet first. The birthing process was more than difficult and although my brother's head finally managed to follow his feet, my mother had lost so much blood that it became clear to the midwife she needed hospital attention. As well as a dangerous loss of blood, the birth had exhausted her so much she had no strength left to push free the placenta and the midwife was unable to remove it. Transport to the hospital was required but the midwife would only arrange for a taxi once the fare had been paid in advance. My father was at work and could not make his way home in time. Thankfully, his larger than life temper and reputation was enough; he made it clear over the telephone that the midwife's own future would be potentially compromised and cut short if his wife and child did not survive. The threat was sufficient to convince her to arrange for a taxi poste haste; just in time, as my mother was informed by the western doctor who attended her. It was yet another near escape from death; one of her many 'cat lives'.

Three girls followed three boys. The first of my two sisters, who arrived next, did not have such a difficult birth, but my mother had been ill with tuberculosis during her pregnancy and had only just completed her course of antibiotics when my eldest sister was born. Neither she, nor her new infant, were in the best of health, nor was their living environment conducive to wellbeing. The stone hut was still intact when the younger of my two sisters visited Hong Kong in the early 1980s.

Amazingly, it had escaped Hong Kong's ceaseless drive to demolish the old to make way for the new, but by then it was surrounded and hemmed in by large, modern buildings. It had survived perhaps because it was made of stone and, being the width of an alleyway meant it could be squeezed in between two buildings and escape destruction. While sturdy, it was small, dark and dank. Cooking was done outside, I hope as far as was possible, away from the open sewer that ran in front of the entrance.

Even for someone such as my mother who had experienced so much poverty and hardship throughout her young life their home in Hung Hom was a difficult place to live, but my parents made do. Alternatives were limited and it was still better than the squatter huts built of wood and metal sheets that filled the hillsides; dwellings that were always at risk from fire and other natural disasters, such as typhoons and heavy rains and where space was cramped and crowded. At least in Hung Hom, there was always the pavement outside the small hut which doubled as a public walkway and a living space during the day and sleeping space during the hot nights.

A traumatic childhood of bereavement and physical want, sold unwillingly into marriage, a failed suicide attempt, the loss of a child; she was a woman who, on the outside was a filial daughter, a compliant wife and an active mother but inside, she was desperate for answers to the meaning of life.

Chapter 6

God and Mahjong

The tug of war of loyalties, combined with a desperate desire for love and affirmation, meant that although her living environment had improved, my mother still struggled inwardly. She had tried to die but failed, now she was very much alive with children that relied on her; yet she didn't want to live. Outwardly, all seemed well, but behind her buoyant exterior was a burning question: "What was the meaning to life?" Buying food, cooking, eating, sleeping, looking after the children, repeat. If this was all there was then life to her seemed pitiful. It was not a life she wanted but there seemed no escape. By 1960, she had four children and since she received no answer to whether there was anything more to life, all she could do was carry on, day upon day, year upon year. To escape the mundane routine of a seemingly futile life, she immersed herself in mahjong.

Each morning, similar to all other housewives of the day, she made her way to the local market. Once groceries had been bought for the day's meals, food prepped and the children dressed and taken care of and her husband at work, she would go and play mahjong. If my father asked her if she had been playing or was going to play, she would always lie. Such was her fixation on mahjong that all else took a back seat.

Like most families, ours has a few, well worn, stock stories that are usually retold at family gatherings. One of these stories illustrates well my mother's life at this time and involves my third brother and a pot of just boiled soup. For those not familiar with Chinese family meals, especially traditional southern Chinese meals, soup is an essential, almost daily, necessity. In a moment of hyper overactivity, my third brother stuffed his school uniform into the pot of soup and in doing so, tipped the scalding hot liquid over himself. In panic, my eldest uncle, who had now arrived from China, ran to get my mother who was sitting at a mahjong table in a neighbour's home:

"Ah Jer, Ah Jer* Fat jai has been scalded!"

Instead of rushing to check on her injured son, her immediate response was to ask whether it was serious, and if not, whether it could wait until she had finished the hand she was playing. Such was

* "Ah Jer" means sister in Cantonese

the hold that it had on her life. She felt bound; tethered to the shore by a mooring rope. No matter what she did, she couldn't escape.

Unknown to my mother however, answers to her existential question was to be forthcoming. My grandmother had been introduced to Jesus and attended a local church. Each time on her return, she enthusiastically encouraged her daughter to go with her to listen to what they had to say. 'I'm not going!' was always the curt response. Undeterred, my grandmother persisted but the reply remained the same.

It seemed that my mother was too hard a case to crack; she needed a direct encounter with God to break through her defences. This was to come when, soon after, on her daily trip to the market, she walked past a kindergarten located on the second floor of a building near her home. Then, as now, such spaces are often used as churches on Sundays since units without a street level frontage are cheaper and can double up as commercial spaces on weekdays and churches on weekends. She knew of the kindergarten as my brothers had attended it. At the same time, she noticed a westerner, wearing a clean white shirt, carrying a briefcase enter the building and go up to the second floor. At that moment, she heard a voice;

"This man is such a good man who believes in Jesus. Why don't you love Jesus?"

The voice was a shock. What followed is best told in my mother's own words:

> "I wondered, why was there a voice? Then, my own heart responded. Right! After I finish buying at the market, I'm going to play my fill of mahjong. Then I'll follow my mother to church. But almost immediately at the same time, I could see myself. I was so filthy. I saw myself as pathetic and dirty as the mud on the ground. Not red or brown, but the black earth like the mud in China. I was pitiful and worthless. That day, I went home and played mahjong the whole day. Thereafter, I never played again. My own brother was confused by the change in me and asked me why I no longer played. Even I didn't know. I had no interest at all in mahjong. It felt as though before I knew the Lord I had been like a ship, tied to the shore by a mooring rope. I floated and swayed but could not escape. Now the rope had been cut by a large knife. One cut; I could sail away. I was free!"

She was free indeed. The following Sunday she went to church and was asked if she loved Jesus. The reply was instantaneous, 'Yes!' and that was it. She was baptised a year later in 1961 with my grandmother. A year later, we were told that we had been successful in our application for one of the new government housing units built at the time. Our circumstances were looking up.

Chapter 7

Yet Another New Beginning

According to figures from the Hong Kong government, by 1950 some 300,000 people were packed into squatter communities. Any housing that managed to remain standing after the war was inevitably jammed full and could not accommodate the staggering numbers of migrants entering the territory after the war and numerous squatter camps sprang up covering vast swathes of land on the rocky hillsides of which Hong Kong Island and much of Kowloon is composed.

Dwellings, built from corrugated tin sheets or any other materials that could be salvaged or scavenged, elbowed each other for air, space and sunlight. Shacks were perched without foundations on the sides of slopes that were prone to landslides during heavy rainfall, while the lack of regulated running water and electricity meant the squatter settlements were a fire and hygiene hazard. Thus, it was that the Hong Kong government instigated a public housing building programme in the 1950s; low cost housing to accommodate the hordes of labourers and workers that had flooded the territory. Demand was huge, so when my parents were told in 1962 that we had been successful in our application and would be one of the first families to move into the newly built Narcissus House on the Ma Tau Wai estate in Kowloon, friends and acquaintances considered us to have struck the jackpot. Narcissus House was completed in 1962 and, as my second brother always proudly reminds us, we were the first occupants of room 415.

The flats all comprised one room with a balcony, kitchen space and wet room that doubled as a toilet and shower at the back. The units were of two sizes, 175.68 sq ft and 245 sq ft. The smaller units were built to accommodate families of five, the second, families of seven and for families of ten or more, two of the smaller units were combined. None of my remaining family can recall whether we were allocated the smaller unit or the mid-sized 245 sq ft living space but, since in 1962 our family consisted of six people and my mother was still young enough to bear more children, it is hoped that our new home was 245 sq ft. Two more children did indeed follow; another daughter in 1963 and a final daughter, myself, in 1965; consistent with the symmetry of each of her earlier children who had arrived in pairs in each location where they had lived. To accommodate six children and two adults in such a small space a cloth was hung as a curtain to separate the single room and foldable canvas beds used which were put away during the day. To put the size of the units into context, a single car garage is approximately 200 sq ft. No wonder lives were lived communally, centred on the large landing onto which our flat faced and which was used as a play space and outdoor sleep area during the summer months.

The improved sanitation and availability of running water on the premises must have seemed like heaven to a busy mother of six children at a time when meals were prepared from scratch three times a day and clothes and nappies still had to be washed by hand. The household of eight was, in reality, one of ten as my grandmother and youngest uncle were permanent fixtures. Tensions persisted, sandwiching wife between mother-in-law and husband, but despite her busy life, once she became a Christian, she came to love reading the Bible and praying, both of which she would do at the end of the day when all her household chores had been done and we children, put to bed.

Being able to read the Bible and other spiritual books was a blessing that supported her throughout her Christian journey but her ability to read at all was another example of her tenacity and inquisitive mind. It is not unusual for Chinese women of my mother's generation to be illiterate. An education outside of the home was not considered necessary or even desirable. Afterall, a girl's life would be constrained by marriage and motherhood; intellectual abilities beyond the practical were considered unnecessary and undesirable. Perhaps, unlike the majority of girls in China at the time, my mother would have been taught how to read and write as she was so loved, but all such hopes faded with the Japanese invasion. None of this deterred my mother. She longed to read and the only way she could learn was to teach herself by sheer force of character and persistence.

Unlike English, Chinese is not made up of a set alphabet. Instead, each word is a 'character' comprising a number of strokes and, in general, needs to be memorised individually. In 2013, the Chinese government published a list of 3,500 most essential characters used in modern Chinese society. A university graduate is expected to have a knowledge of 8,000 characters. It is unlikely she knew as many as 8,000 but she knew enough to enable her to read, especially the Bible. Nor did age diminish her desire to learn. Well into her eighties she would stare at English words on television or hospital signs and medication bottles and ask me to confirm letters in a spelling, just in case she got them wrong, or she would mull a word over in her mind and then surprise me with a question on a spelling or pronunciation that she had been working on for days or weeks. It was a strategy that she had used as a young woman when she first tried to read.

My grandmother, who herself could not read, at first dismissed and disparaged her daughter's attempts when she saw my mother staring at newspapers, trying to work out a meaning. She would use the subtitles when she went to the cinema, street names and advertising hoardings as well as newspaper headlines and ask friends, family or even strangers for individual words which she then committed to memory. Piece by piece, like a jigsaw puzzle, she would then try to fit words she knew into a sentence to decipher the meaning of new characters. If she was really stuck, as a means of last resort, she would ask a friendly neighbour.

It was arduous work, but her tenacity paid off and she was able to shock my grandmother when one day she read a newspaper headline out aloud and explained the article to her astonished mother. The ability to read gave her a means to feed her intellectual curiosity and spiritual hunger. Her love of the Bible remained till her dying day and one of my enduring images of my mother is of her sitting in her rocking chair by the window, reading her Bible, early in the morning or late at night. It was a source of supreme comfort and joy to her.

Her inner transformation had been paralleled by our family's external circumstances. No longer tied to mahjong, she found a new joy in life. She herself recalls astonishment at her own change. If she saw a stranger drop a bag of rice, she would stop and help them scoop it up or she would help carry shopping for neighbours. Gone was the annoyingly brashy girl of her youth. For the next six years, life, though busy, was smooth. She still had to navigate between her husband and mother, but just as life had settled into an easier rhythm, change was to arrive again when my father's enterprising spirit led him to accept an offer of a job in London. Fearless as ever, he sought a future for his family in a wholly new and unknown environment. He left in October of 1965. Eighteen months later, when he felt settled enough, he arranged for the rest of his family to follow him. The remaining seven members of the family arrived in London in May of 1967. My mother was thirty-six years old.

Chapter 8

Spiritual Hunger

Our first lodgings in the UK were rented from a Chinese lady whom we called, Aunty Bishop. My father's employer had only been willing to sign on as a sponsor for our family if he did not have to provide us with housing. Six children and a wife were, in his mind and that of every other landlord we came across, far too many to accommodate. Thankfully, the pastor of the newly formed Chinese congregation at St Martin-in-the-Fields in London, Pastor Li Shiu Ying, was able to connect us to a Chinese lady who took lodgers. Aunty Bishop was willing to take a chance on us and squeezed all eight of us into two rooms on the first floor of her three storied house in Finsbury Park; one small box room and the other, a larger bedroom. She was also the one who gave the children our English names. We stayed for three crammed months in London before moving to Southport, a seaside town in the Northwest of England. A friend of my father's, also from his home province, Shandong , wanted to open a restaurant and was in need of a chef to run his kitchen and so, in the hope of better accommodation in a smaller town, we moved.

Unfortunately, just as in London, finding a place to stay for a family of eight newly arrived Chinese immigrants was difficult. For three pounds a week, we ended up in a derelict house that, by today's standards and even by the standards of the time, would be listed as near condemned. The house had been empty for three years and had no heating or hot water. The stove and oven were so encrusted with dirt and rust that Dad spent three days cleaning it before he was able to roast a chicken for the whole family.

On the third day of our arrival my mother experienced the first of many adversities she was to encounter after leaving Hong Kong. Since there was no boiler, hot water was heated on a stove in the kitchen in a large pot. Being the strongest, my eldest brother was tasked with the job of carrying the large pot of just-boiled water up the stairs to the bathroom where the rest of the family had congregated, but just as he arrived at the top step, he caught his foot and tripped. The heavy pot was dropped onto the landing and like a tidal wave in slow motion, the scalding hot water rose in a sheet, curved over the heads of everyone in the room and landed on my second sister who was at the farthest corner of the room. Not a single drop touched any other person.

With no phone available, my second brother ran to fetch my father who was at work, while my mother frantically tried to cut away my sister's clothes and doused her, ineffectually, with bottles of Chinese medicine she had brought from Hong Kong. My sister, who was only four at the time, was rushed to Southport Infirmary. Everything beneath her eyes was covered in blisters. We had been in England only a few months and my sister could not speak English and so the kindly nurses allowed my mother to stay at her bedside. With no language skills herself my mother could only sit by her bed and pray. During those long days and nights she remembered the kindness of nurses who gave her cups of tea and one particular nurse who supplied her with a boiled egg when she noticed that my mother had not eaten through the day and had no money to buy any food. She had entered the hospital praying to God that Jesus would move the hands of the doctors to heal her daughter, but through the night as she read the Bible, Zechariah chapter 4 verse 6 spoke to her:

"Not by might, nor by power but by my Spirit says the Lord Almighty."

It was an 'aha' moment. She realised she could go straight to God the Father and she did. Such was God's assurance and such was her belief in the promise of God's word that immediately, the weight that had wrapped itself around her heart like a stone was lifted. With her husband at work, she had five young children at home on their own and a daughter in hospital, but she knew that God would look after us. At that moment, my mother experienced the reality of God's presence and truth and was filled with thankfulness. Her prayers were indeed answered. Amazingly, my sister suffered no lasting scarring save for a very small piece of skin on her leg which chaffed when she walked. Indeed, if anything, she has the best skin complexion of us all!

Both mother and daughter spent 28 days in hospital; days spent by my mother reading the Bible. It was an unforeseen blessing. Despite the circumstances, she was always grateful for that short period of her life when she could spend whole days and nights pouring over scripture, praying and reading and re-reading her Bible without distraction to meet her spiritual hunger. It was a time of plenty for the times of famine that would come when life became so busy that she hardly had time to eat and breathe, never mind read and pray.

When I was older, she would frequently pop out obscure Bible verses or surprise me with the detail with which she could recall biblical events. Whenever she did so, she would come alive, glowing with excitement. The Bible was precious and her appetite for God's Word, boundless. She mastered reading but was never able to write and so had to memorise everything that she wanted to retain. I often wonder what she would have achieved had she had the opportunities open to girls of today.

Sugar People Street

While in London my mother had been able to worship at St Martin-in-the-Fields which had a recently formed Chinese congregation which met in the basement of the church but when we arrived in Southport, there was no such corresponding place of worship for Chinese speakers and since my mother at that stage spoke not a word of English, joining an English congregation was not an option.

Unlike today, the Chinese population in England and Wales was much smaller. The census of 2011 shows that there were 393,141 ethnic Chinese in England and Wales (now, most certainly more) but in 1961, according to census figures obtained by the Society for Anglo Chinese Understanding, the figure stood at 38,750, skyrocketing in the next ten years to 96,030 in 1971. When we arrived in 1967, it was unusual to bump into a Chinese person walking randomly along the street, especially outside of London.

Undeterred, my mother, with her limited six years of Church teaching and Christian experience, decided that if she could not find a church in which to worship, we would worship at home. To that end, every Sunday morning she would go from room to room, chivvying her sleepy children out of bed so she could organise a family worship time. My father did not go to work on Sunday mornings but he, like the rest of us, needed a lot of persuasion to get up. She would go from room to room rounding up husband and children. In her own words, it was like a merry go round. One would wake only to fall back asleep; another would be pulled up then plop back into bed. Once all seven were fully awake, she placed us in two rows, youngest at the front, eldest with herself and our father, at the back. Standing, she had us sing, pray and read a portion of the Bible. Her children, still young, of course had little say in the matter, but I am still amazed that my father was a willing participant, sacrificing his much needed lie-in for a morning home worship service.

After nine months of family worship, a friend of my father's bumped into him at the restaurant where he worked and offered to drive us to a Chinese grocery store in Liverpool, a large city about 45 minutes away by car. While there, the friend drove past Chinatown, which in the 1960s was the only other established Chinese community outside of London and pointed out the location of a Chinese Church. He knew enough to inform my mother that Sunday meetings took place in the late afternoon, around 4pm. My mother was so excited to hear this news, she stuck her head out of the car window to try and establish the exact location but the car whizzed past all too quickly. How would she find it again? She had no address, no telephone and could not speak the language. Despite such handicaps, undeterred, and displaying that impressive determination that had featured throughout her life, she decided to take a train into Liverpool that coming Sunday and look for it herself.

To give herself enough time to find the church, she left the house at 11am and arrived in Liverpool with myself and my third brother in tow. I have since walked the distance between Lime Street station to Nelson Street, where the church was located, many, many times. The distance is not great, less than 15 minutes, but for my mother, it could have been 15 hours.

She had no idea which way to go. My brother, who knew a few words of English, had the bright idea of transliterating the Chinese for Chinatown into English. In Cantonese, Chinatown sounds like: 'tan' sugar, 'yan' people, 'gai' street: Sugar People Street. Needless to say, Mother knew that the translation was wrong, but she always recounted this story with a laugh. At the time, it was no laughing matter. She spent hours wandering around Liverpool with two children in tow but would not give up. I can no longer recall the event, but I could not have been a helpful addition to the search and most likely hindered than helped. When it seemed that she would have to give up, it was then that the third passing stranger came into her life. Although Liverpool had a Chinatown, in the 1960s Chinese people were by no means prevalent on the streets. Even in the 1970s and 80s, when I was a teenager, I was often considered a novelty by people I met. So it was that when my mother saw a passing Chinese man, she grabbed hold of him to ask for directions. Miraculously, he told us he was a student and that he was going to the very same place. He led us to the very door of the church, but my mother never saw him again. Was he an angel sent to guide us? Whether an angel in human form or just a plain human, he played the part of an angel. Would I have had the tenacity to continue for so many hours, with two children, one aged only three and the other ten. God saw my mother's spiritual hunger and met her in her need.

The church we arrived at was located at 20 Nelson Street and had started life as the Chinese Gospel Mission in the mid 1950s with links to Gladys Aylward, a missionary to China made famous by the film, The Inn of the Sixth Happiness. When we first arrived, there was no formal ordained pastor but worship services in Chinese were held. The congregation moved out of the premises in the 1970s and the building has since been used as a Chinese restaurant, but I retain vague memories of making mud pies in the backyard and eating egg and cress sandwiches made by Aunty Joyce, the English lady who taught us Sunday School.

The church has, through the years, undergone a number of changes, in name, location and leadership, as has the size of the Chinese Christian community in Liverpool. Today, there are at least five Chinese congregations scattered in and around the city. Mud pies, in any part of church services, are no longer acceptable but I am glad to say that in any circumstance, for myself at least, egg and cress sandwiches remain much appreciated.

Chapter 9

A Breach of Trust

God had encouraged my mother's faith when He had reassured her of my sister's recovery during those anxious days at hospital. Although she had been a Christian only six years when she arrived in Britain, instead of wavering, her faith was her bulwark through the difficulties she was to encounter. One of her many qualities was a resolve to never base her trust in God's love on the behaviour of those around her. It was a resolve that was sorely tested when a business decision left our family on the edge of a precipice.

We stayed in Southport until my father found an opportunity to operate his own restaurant which he found in Liverpool. The business was located near Chinatown but had been closed due to health and safety violations. Although my father had the skills to run the kitchen he needed a partner to be the legal owner since he was still in need of a sponsor for his work visa. In any event, he did not have sufficient funds to get the business up and running on his own; a promised loan did not materialise and my parents could borrow only five hundred pounds from a friend, enough to pay only for renovation works. Conveniently at the time, a young, fresh college graduate with a new expectant wife was also looking for a business opportunity. It was agreed that he would deal with the finances and paperwork and be the legal owner while my father and mother arranged everything else.

It took weeks to clear out the building to make it habitable and commercially usable. The first floor above the restaurant had been an opium den and my mother recalls removing mounds of rubbish including human excrement. With my parents providing the labour and the culinary expertise the restaurant became a thriving, prosperous venture. Of the six children, those old enough to help also chipped in. My eldest brother in the kitchen and my second brother at the front of the restaurant. My parents cleaned the floors, washed the tablecloths, cooked and prepared the food. For a while, all seemed well but after about a year after the restaurant began trading we were to find ourselves once again near desperation.

The restaurant opened its doors in August of 1968 and did roaring trade, so much so that less than a year later, they were able to support an extra pair of hands in the kitchen. Mr Tse* was a fellow northerner from China who asked my father for help when his employer had confiscated his passport. The passport was eventually recovered with the help of the police, but since he no longer had a job to return to, it was suggested that he stay and work with my father in the kitchen of the new restaurant. Unfortunately for my parents, he also took the opportunity to undercut my father from the business by coming to an agreement with the other partner, with whom he had ingratiated himself, to remove my father by offering to buy-him out.

With no notice my father was offered three thousand pounds for his share of the business and asked to leave. Perhaps there may have been an option for further discussion, but my father was a hot-tempered man. He saw how he had been backstabbed by a friend he had helped and stormed out. For years, whenever the name of the man he thought had been a friend was mentioned, he would grow red with anger. Mr Tse's name could not be spoken in Dad's presence.

It is a measure of how much God changed my father that, a few years before his death, he was able to fully forgive the man who had so betrayed his trust and friendship. It was during a particular special church service where friends and family were invited, that my dad spotted the then elderly

---

* His name has been changed

man in the congregation. Without hesitation, Dad walked over to him and shook his hand. The man was so moved that he cried. His wife, who knew nothing of their past history, asked why he was crying like a child. Even my mother was shocked. God had so changed my father that he no longer felt any animosity towards a man whom he had raged against for most of thirty years.

On the face of it, the buy-out was not unreasonable. My father was given money for his share, but it had been done without consultation by two people both my parents considered friends; one whom my father had tried to help and the other, a Christian leader whom my mother looked up to. It was also a sign that they had conspired behind his back. On a more practical level, my father was now without employment with six children and a wife to feed and clothe, without access to state funds and reliant only on the three thousand pounds he had received as payoff. All other savings and credit had been used up in the move to the UK and in getting the business started.

While my father seethed in anger, my mother felt deeply betrayed and used. They had sweated blood and tears to get the business going and were now left with a future that seemed very bleak. My mother knew no English, had no support system and the few friends she knew had betrayed her. Worse still, our visas were near to expiry and my father needed a sponsor in the form of an employer to secure a renewal. It was truly a desperate time.

Fish Heads and Boiled Cabbage

It would have been easy for my mother to speak of how she felt and ask for an explanation from the Christian friend who had quite a high standing in the Chinese community. But once again, she wanted to honour God and for the rest of her life, spoke about her feelings of hurt and hardships that followed to only a few people and never in a judgmental, negative way.

For a whole year, with no income and afraid to eat too much into their savings, my father picked up discarded fish heads from the rubbish tip of the main fish market in the city which my mother cooked with cabbages, the cheapest vegetable available at the time. I was too young to remember the monotonous diet, but my brothers became so sick of fish heads and cabbage they would routinely puke at the thought of them.

The most pressing problem though, was the work visa. My father's friends in London suggested that he return down south where they would sign the papers required for him to renew his visa and obtain an extension. Miraculously, without even asking, when the papers were returned from the passport office, it was stamped with the right of abode. He no longer needed an employer; he was free to start his business in his own name.

The opportunity came when an acquaintance was willing to sell a going concern and contacted my parents. The business was an existing one and there would be no need to buy equipment or clean out opium dens as they had in their first ill-fated venture. Everything was agreed, the sale price was four thousand, eight hundred pounds but just as the papers were to be signed my mother was told by the seller that only half would be paid to the solicitor dealing with the sale; the other half would be paid to him directly.

Pen in hand, my mother paused.

When asked the reason for this arrangement, she was told that it was for tax avoidance purposes. She had not been a Christian for long, but she was intent on honouring God and told the seller she could not walk with him on such a dark path. The man was surprisingly quite understanding. He even said that he knew she went to church and that it would be a poor witness to her God and so, to my dad's fury, the sale fell through.

My mother had held onto her convictions but there was a price to pay: there remained eight mouths to feed. In desperation, she fell on her knees in prayer.

The verses of Psalm 73:2-4 became very real to her:

"But as for me, my feet had almost stumbled, my steps
had nearly slipped.
For I was envious of the arrogant
when I saw the prosperity of the wicked.
For they have no pangs till death,
their bodies are fat and sleek."

It was a hard lesson and would not be the last time that she was willing to honour God despite the price she would have to pay. Contrary to how some may preach, staying faithful does not always bring prosperity in this life. My mother's life was a clear example. Choosing to honour God may bring suffering, but through the pain, she held fast and stayed faithful.

Finally, after nearly a year, another opportunity appeared when we were told of another restaurant up for sale. It was cheap: one thousand, four hundred and fifty pounds and, because it was so cheap, there was no need to make under the table payments. Low prices of course come with a reason. The property boasted only a few curry bowls, an old fridge and a clapped out stove, but God had already made arrangements. Another restaurant had recently gone bankrupt and were looking to sell equipment. My parents were asked if they were interested. For two hundred pounds they could take as much kitchen equipment as they could manage: tables and chairs, plates and cutlery, even furniture from the dormitory for the workers. It was heaven sent. We were still living in a rented house and had little furniture of our own. The new business at Marlborough Road had accommodation on floors above the restaurant and could house the whole family. My parents, with my three brothers, spent three days and two nights dismantling everything and moving it to the new restaurant. At the end of the three days, my father was so exhausted he fell asleep in the bathtub.

The new venture opened in May 1970. The restaurant was located a good few miles away from Chinatown in a far from salubrious neighbourhood, but despite initial confrontations with local gangs and troublemakers and lack of cash to even pay for a first crate of coca cola, business thrived. My father soon dispensed with any offerings of English favourites and stuck to his Beijing style of high-end cuisine at affordable prices; it was a big hit. The restaurant opened for lunch and dinner, entertaining a constant flow of activity and people, both in the dining rooms below and the living quarters above. It became so popular that customers would be known to wait sitting on the double stairs that led up to the dining area.

Quite apart from the ceaseless activity in the restaurant below, the number of people my parents hosted for the three short years we lived above the restaurant at Marlborough Road seem to have been endless. Somehow, crammed into the living space was my youngest uncle, whom my parents sponsored to study in the UK, an entire family of six that had emigrated from Hong Kong, and a young Chinese student who I remember most for introducing me to the concept of atoms and subatomic particles. To accommodate all these additional people, my father built a number of partitioned rooms which were little more than boards of plywood stood upright at 90 degree angles from each other with a door attached. There may not even have been ceilings! Health and Safety has since come a long way.

Chapter 10

Being Authentic

My mother had been a Christian for only six years before arriving in Britain. She had attended no Bible studies or any other form of Christian instruction other than the sermons she managed to listen to on Sundays. Even these opportunities were fraught with difficulty. There were no childcare facilities for nursing mothers or mothers with small children and she would frequently have to stand outside the meeting room with myself and my sister, straining to listen while we wriggled and cried. At night she would pore over her Bible, painstakingly piecing together the words she had learnt. With the same tenacity she had displayed as a young woman living hand to mouth in post war torn Hong Kong she now pursued, with irrepressible spiritual hunger, the truth of the gospel: the good news, that she was loved and that she had a Heavenly Father.

She had a multitude of questions but had no chance to ask but now, having now moved to Liverpool she finally had access to a pastor who was willing and able to answer and address her questions, one of which was; "What was it to be a Christian?" Was she a Christian? In answer, her pastor held out his hands: imagine two silver coins, was his answer. When thrown to the ground, the coin that is fully silver, without adulteration, will ring clear and true while the fake coin will give a dull thud. My mother was always ready to mull over spiritual truths and as she asked God the fuller meaning of this illustration she realised that it was in her response to life's vicissitudes and challenges that the veracity of her faith would be shown: what cost was she willing to bear? In her life and in her work, she would have to keep checking that there were no adulterations; she would have to keep throwing the coin onto the ground to test its purity.

It was a lesson she held onto for the rest of her life and one that she needed to ensure that her actions always honoured God, none more so than in her determination to ensure that her family's business practices were irreproachable. She had stood firm in her refusal to allow Dad to buy the business that asked for under the table payments but even though occurrences of tax avoidance were common. On the occasion my parents sought to buy a large commercial sized fridge the seller refused to accept a cheque. He wanted cash to avoid declaring

VAT, a form of business tax. To compound the dilemma, when my mother protested that although the seller did not wish to declare VAT they did, he offered to give her a written receipt so my parents could reclaim the taxation on the item. My mother was shocked with the very idea. How could she add sin upon sin. Not declaring was bad enough but how could she claim for something she had not spent? She refused the purchase.

Unlike his wife, my father had no objections to such a transaction and was livid with anger and exasperation at her stubbornness. While her husband jumped up and down in frustration, she too raged, but her tears were those of anger at the impunity of evil in the world. On her way home, she was furious with a righteous anger, crying hot tears of frustration to God. So vehement were her emotions she was completely taken unawares by the sudden stillness that overwhelmed her heart when she arrived home and was about to open her front door. God had seen her tears and the turmoil of her heart and in His love, replaced her anger with complete, unexpected peace.

A determination to stand firm, even over seemingly trifling matters, was for her, a matter of principle. She understood that challenges in life came not as large, overt problems, but small ones; small problems or cracks that, if allowed to widen, would soon become a gaping hole into which she would fall. She was determined not to allow that to happen and would often quote the example of the sale of alcohol on their restaurant premises.

Profit margins are far higher on the sale of beverages than in food and it was in their interests to sell as much alcohol as possible. Their initial restaurant in Marlborough Road eventually gave way to larger premises and with it came a licence to sell alcohol. By law, the bar closed at 11pm but my mother would be scrupulous in refusing to take any further orders after 10:45pm, despite the urging of customers and even staff.

To try and circumvent this problem, customers resorted to creative measures: "Mrs Lau, teapot," they would say, holding up the pot and pointing to it to ensure their suggestion, that alcohol be poured into the pot, was understood. "Against the law" would be my mother's response. It may have seemed a small matter, but she held firm, even willing to offend customers. In her mind, offending man was better than offending God.

The same held true for Sunday trading. Normally, weekends are the most lucrative for food and beverage businesses, but she was insistent that the restaurant closed on Sundays to allow the family to attend church. In this, as with the sale of alcohol, she was adamant, despite my father's objections, but God honours those that honour Him. To my father's, and everyone else's surprise, earnings remained the same even when they no longer opened on Sunday. God had honoured her intention of not allowing any gaps to appear in her life that would widen into a chasm.

Patient Waiting

"In whatever I do, my main aim is not to injure or harm the name of my Heavenly Father."

Such was her overriding consideration in everything she did. She knew that she could not share the good news of Jesus to her family if her life did not reflect the very gospel she sought to communicate. Although God changed my father dramatically in his later years, he was not an ideal husband. Even though he was loyal and generous, he was a man with an explosive hot temper, easily angered and not adverse to violence. He was also a man who drank heavily, smoked and gambled and had done so since his teenage years.

From the start of their marriage, he would often go gambling in the evenings after finishing work. Since he never took a key, he would expect her to wait up for him. When we moved to a two storied house in Liverpool, if she nodded off before he returned, he would throw small stones or coins up at the window of the front bedroom.

If he disappeared from the restaurant during opening hours, she knew he would be at a gambling den in Chinatown. Whenever this happened, she would leave the restaurant in the hands of a reliable employee and drive to collect him, all the while praying in the car that she would not dishonour God by shouting at him or abuse him in any way in front of friends or employees. To do her justice, I never heard her speak badly of my father even though she had plenty of reasons to do so. Her overriding desire was not to violate God's name and in this, God honoured her heart's desire by giving her a supernatural ability to hold her tongue and her temper when it came to her husband and his failings. Instead of relying on her own methods, she turned to her Heavenly Father and spent hours in tearful prayer on her husband's behalf.

It turned out that her silent patience was more effective than hot tempered shouting and nagging. As my father's friends confirmed years after his death, as soon as my father saw his wife enter the room when he was gambling, he would turn pale and rivulets of sweat would begin to run down his face. Not wanting to humiliate him in front of his friends, she would inevitably only say in a quiet voice, 'Father, let's go'. She would then wait outside in the street while he finished his hand.

Even in the car returning to the restaurant, she was able to hold her tongue and not berate him despite her inner struggle. She knew my father's character and that conflict was counterproductive. Only on one occasion, she asked him why he needed to gamble. His answer was instructive: he himself did not know. "I don't want to go, but it seems my feet just take me there without me knowing." Gambling had a deep hold on him and it would have continued until a turning point came in his life.

On one particularly bad night, he lost three thousand pounds. In the 1970s, this was a lot of money. My mother only found out when a gambling buddy told his wife who then told my mother. She was distraught. How much time and work did it take to earn that amount of money and he had lost it in one night. For three days she struggled within herself whether to speak to him or not. On the third day, she sat in the car and heard these words come to her:

"Money doesn't belong to you. Don't be a slave to money. If money belongs to you, money should be your slave."

She was amazed at the words she heard. Although she helped run the business, she intentionally did not manage the money. If she did not have any dealings with the money, why then, she thought to herself, did she need to agonise and struggle over these three thousand pounds? If she did hold onto the money then the money was her slave and she could do with it as she liked. Either way, she had no need to be under the power of money.

It was like a heavy weight was lifted from her heart. This event was the catalyst that helped Dad to slowly disengage from gambling. He gambled less and less, eventually stopping altogether. His smoking followed suit and he finally stopped drinking. He was indeed a changed man.

Chapter 11

Dealing with Forgiveness

Mother and Daughter

Central to my mother's life was her relationship with her own mother: it was also the one relationship that caused her the deepest pain. My grandmother was not a deep-thinking woman; until disaster befell the family, she had not needed to concern herself with anything more onerous than dressmaking and theatre seating arrangements. It had been a cosseted and comfortable life. Little wonder then that she was completely unprepared for the life of toil and want that faced her when she was left as the only adult member of a previously prosperous family.

I knew my maternal grandmother only when she was in her old age and comfortably ensconced in her tidy government flat on the eastern side of Kowloon. Despite the availability of refrigeration since the late 1960s, she would still keep food in a small, dark cubbyhole used as a pantry. On my first visit, she whisked out a plate of Chinese rice cake that had been kept in careful storage since the Lunar New Year (celebrated in late January or early February) - my visit took place in June. My British stomach was saved by an alert friend whose vigorous eye winking persuaded me to forgo the proffered treat. She did not often refer to her early years in Hong Kong and hardly ever of her life in China. It is understandable that she preferred to focus on the son of her old age and the life she now had, or perhaps my language skills were not up to the task but, whatever the reason, deep discussions of an emotionally traumatic past were never entered upon.

The same restraint was not the case between my mother and her two youngest daughters. She shared freely her memories of her childhood and life in Hong Kong and, as we grew older, of her experiences in the UK. When we were younger, before she retired, she had so little time and opportunity to spend with us that she would take every opportunity to share life experiences as a way of teaching us biblical truths.

As we grew older and my father less inflexible, general biblical sharing would often take place over the dining table. Prior to this, up to my late teens, I was still under the misapprehension that Chinese culture forbade any communication at all while eating since for my father, food and its consumption took such precedence no talk was allowed at all while we ate. There were to be no distractions from the important business of eating. Being the youngest, my objections to what I saw as an unreasonable and illogical mandate were never heeded, leaving me to protest in silent impotence while the rest of my family would focus on studied eating.

An unlooked for outcome of my mother's willingness to share with those disposed to listen was an appreciation of how her relationship with her own mother shaped her fears and behaviour. The loss of her grandparents and father at such a young age was compounded by the actions of a mother who undoubtedly loved her, but who was never very wise.

She was unable to comprehend the impact on a small girl, who had so recently suffered so much loss, being left overnight to guard an empty house with only the recently deceased corpse of my great grandfather for company; nor could she appreciate the conflicted loyalties and problems she created between her daughter and son-in-law through her liberal treatment of my father's generosity. Most importantly, she was never able to grasp how deeply her daughter felt regarding the origins of her marriage. "Sold like a piggy at market" is the phrase my mother used. Feelings of loss, rejection and abandonment were deeply embedded and it took many years before she was finally able to speak of these experiences without tears but healing took place and it started soon after her arrival in Liverpool.

My mother's most formative spiritual years took place in the early 1970s. The presence of a pastor and his wife who took an actual interest in her spiritual wellbeing was like spring water to dry, parched ground. It was this same pastor that gave her the illustration of the silver coins as a teaching aid; a lesson she never forgot, and this same pastor who was the first to direct her to an insight into her own conflicted emotions towards my grandmother; unresolved feelings that revealed themselves when, on a pastoral visit, he asked my mother directly:

"Mrs Lau, Mrs Lau, are there any sins in your life?"

My mother was shocked. Her initial reaction was to ask:

"What sin do I have? I love my husband, my family. I don't steal or lie or covet. What sin do I have?"

But the very next moment came the awareness of her anger, indeed, hate that she harboured against her mother; the shocking realisation that she loved her but also hated her in equal measure. Yet she was confused: how could she hate someone for whom she would forgo her own food and the very clothes on her back? Why did she feel this way? The pastor's answer was direct:

"You have mixed up hate with love."

She had used human love and in that human love was also mixed in hate. The two emotions were equally strong and she had been unable to discern between the two.

My mother understood instantly. In her own words, the realisation burnt out the poison of hate. For myself, I must confess it took some time to comprehend the pastor's words. Was it her desperation to love and be loved that in trying so hard to please her mother she had interchanged love and hate in a mishmash of tormented emotions? As soon as she released these previously unrecognized feelings, her life became different. It still took many more years before she could consider herself fully healed but she was now able to love without the contamination of buried hate.

Husband and Wife

Her feelings towards my father however were far more straightforward. She did not hate my father, even during her darkest moments in the first few years of her marriage, but she was angry. Her anger was primarily directed at her mother who had sold her and then, at my father. Even when her anger towards my father resolved, she remained angry towards my grandmother; anger which tussled with hate until God shone a light into her conflicted emotions. At around the same time she realised that her relationship with her mother was that of a love/hate relationship, she also realised that her relationship with my father had been one of fear. In the early years of her marriage, she had yielded to him out of fear when submission should have been out of love.

He was a large man who broached no contradiction and whose word, at home, was law. Their relationship improved over time, first with the arrival of children and then, after my mother became a Christian. In her own words, she understood how to love him, but life was still difficult. Even when she was seriously ill there was no respite from looking after the children and all the housework. On one occasion in Hong Kong, she was so ill that she felt there was no alternative but to ask my father to help by washing a few dishes so the children could eat. His response was that she should buy a take-out; but of course, with no disposable items at the time, crockery still needed to be washed. Even near death brought no help. Seeking medical help in those days, as now, was expensive and not undertaken lightly but she knew she needed to see a doctor when she became ill with a raging fever. Despite being delirious she still had to take the children to my grandmother (my grandmother deemed it unnecessary to make her way to her daughter's home) before she sought help from a doctor who advised her she needed to be admitted to Kowloon hospital for what was later discovered to be tuberculosis. With no one to talk to (her brother was then still in China) and no help or understanding from either husband or mother, it is little wonder that she harboured such anger and resentment.

My father however, was not an unkindly man; he was merely a man of his time, who approached life with a can-do, fearless attitude and a large dose of generosity. My mother would tell me stories of when, still a poorly paid apprentice chef in China, he found a beggar and took him in from off the streets, giving him a place to sleep next to one of the many large kitchen stoves that remained warm with residual heat through the freezing northern Chinese nights. The beggar was an opium addict from a good family. My father had no money to give him to help him return home and so spent nights drying discarded shrimp shells that he collected from the restaurant kitchen which he then sold. Post war China was a poor, economically ravished place and such items found ready buyers who used the dried discarded shells to flavour soup. He eventually saved enough money to buy the young man a ticket for his home town and was rewarded months later by the gratitude of the young man's elderly father, who made the trip to the big city to thank Dad for giving him back a son that he had thought dead.

Towards his children, he was always generous. Even when he gambled in Hong Kong before we left for Britain, he would always keep in his back pocket a twenty Hong Kong dollar note (today, equivalent to just under two pounds sterling) so that, win or lose, he would have money to buy fried chicken and cakes as a treat for our breakfast on his return home.

My father had been baptised in Hong Kong in his thirties but, as he himself admitted later, like most things in his life, the Christian faith was not something he took seriously. There was no indication that his baptism made any impact on his life. As to his wife's faith, he was neither encouraging nor discouraging. He understood its fundamental importance to my mother but until his later years when God changed him, there were never any meaningful conversations between them regarding Christianity. As a child and later, a young adult, I never saw, even remotely, any possibility that my father could be changed from what I saw as engrained stubbornness, but oh ye of little faith! My mother continued to pray for his salvation and unlike her doubting daughter, knew her Heavenly Father could move even the hardest of hearts: she never gave up on him. In fact, it was her commitment to my father that was the cause of her return from a Near Death Experience.

Although on the outside she looked healthy, lifelong hardships had resulted in a number of physical ailments, one of which was a weak heart: she took medication for a heart complaint up until her death. She had also suffered a number of heart attacks and it was during one of these that she experienced what we would now call a Near Death Experience.

On her way to hospital in an ambulance she saw a brilliant white light and found herself in the most beautiful of places, a landscape full of trees. With tears in her eyes, she would say that the beauty was indescribable as was the inner peace she experienced. She knew that Jesus was present and calling to her and she was willing to go, but a sudden recollection of my father who was, as yet, an unbeliever, jolted her: she was not yet ready to leave us.

I was too young to be present during this illness but the joy she exuded when faced with the possibility of joining her Father in Heaven was something I saw first hand on two occasions. Once when I accompanied her in an ambulance to the hospital after yet another heart attack, and the final time, the night she passed away. On the first of these occurrences, her fears for my father had now eased and she was more than willing, eager in fact, to meet her maker. In the ambulance, she radiated joy as she began singing hymns, frustrating the efforts of the paramedics who tried to place an oxygen mask over her mouth.

By the time we reached the A&E department she was crying but they were tears of joy. Nurses and doctors alike thought her tears were those of pain and in their kindness kept asking me where her pain was located. It was with acute embarrassment that I had to tell them that they were tears of joy because she thought she was dying. Here I was, telling them that my mother was singing praises and crying tears of joy in anticipation of the very thing they were trying to prevent: death. Little wonder then, the strange looks from nurses and doctors; but what could I do? She was indeed convulsed with joy but again, it was the thought of leaving my father alone that deflated her anticipation of heaven. In the event, it was not yet time. She had first to help my father through his last days before she could experience both the pain and joy of her own departure.

Such was the richness of my mother's experiences of God that her glorious glimpse of heaven was not the only time that she was given a taste of God's glory. In the early 1970s, at around the same time that she realised she needed to deal with her conflicted emotions towards her mother, she was also seeking a deeper experience of God. She would ask of herself why, when others spoke of God's love as sweet, for her, it did not seem so flavourful. As she expressed it, she felt like an outsider to God's love. It was with these words that she came in prayer to God and even as she asked it, before the last word left her mouth, she had an experience like an explosion: it felt as intense as oil and water hitting a hot wok together. She was so shocked that she fell, her whole body collapsing to the floor. It was then, as she prayed, that she saw an image of Jesus. Eventually, she managed to crawl down the stairs one step at a time and call her pastor. "You have seen God's glory" was his only response. It was an experience that she treasured throughout her life and which helped her through times even when they seemed too dark to navigate.

Eventually however, my mother's faithfulness and perseverance was rewarded; my father did finally commit himself to Jesus and was baptised on 3rd March, 1996, four years shy of his eightieth birthday. His baptism was the culmination of many years of prayer and witness by my mother and others. As he testified during his baptism, he admitted that God had been waiting a long time for him. When they first retired, he would complain to my mother that she was never at home and always in church. Her response was the same as it had been throughout their marriage.

> "Yes, I have two responsibilities. Only after I
> have looked after you well that I go to church.
> I am God's child."

To which he had no reply. She had indeed looked after him well.

Chapter 12

More Lives than a Cat

One of the most amazing things about my mother was the multitude of health problems she faced. She remained mentally, fully alert to her last breath but became increasingly debilitated. For the last two years of her life she was unable to leave the house on her own or walk more than a few steps without great effort, but her many health issues, far from drawing her away from God, drew her closer. It is impossible to list the number of times she needed hospitalisation, from heart attacks, knee operations, slipped discs, ulcers, kidney and gall bladder stones, sepsis (multiple times), fractured hip, superbug infections (picked up from her recurrent hospital stays) and burst blood vessels in the brain.

As well as the alien-like lumps on her shin which persisted until her 80s, she also, for nearly twenty years, wore a girdle, reinforced with two stainless steel plates, as support for her back. In her 40s she suffered a slipped disc, most likely from the heavy physical labour she had to undergo on a daily basis. The doctor advised that an operation was too dangerous and instead prescribed for her an orthopaedic girdle. The plates were each two inches wide and about eight to nine inches long, slipped vertically along the back of the girdle on either side of the spine.

She wore this back support for nearly twenty years, removing it only when she slept. If she had lived another life and not needed to work eighteen to twenty hour, physically demanding days she would perhaps not have needed to wear it for such long periods of time, but that was not an option and so we became accustomed to her figure standing ramrod straight, as she said, like a Roman soldier, unable to bend. If anything fell on the floor, those around her automatically picked it up: we knew she could not. And yet, it was yet more evidence of God's favour upon her and her own dogged persistence that eventually, she was able to stretch, bend and in the end, be more flexible than me. She did not take this for granted and it took courage to remove the girdle after nearly two decades, with no proof that her spine had healed; yet she was determined to do so.

It is possible that the disc had by then self-healed but an unexpected by-product of wearing the girdle for so many hours a day was muscle wastage in her back and abdomen. In her early 60s she made the decision to try and live without the girdle in order to give herself greater mobility. In this, as with all things, she trusted in her Heavenly Father to supply her with the ability to endure the initial pain and painful it was to begin with, but God did not fail her and by the time she reached her 80s no one would have ever known, herself included, that she had ever had a back problem.

She herself was quick to point out that, whilst she asked, God never healed all her ailments. For the last ten years of her life, she suffered excruciating pain from a complications stemming from a replaced hip joint and severe arthritis in her legs but other times saw miraculous moments of healing. One such healing took place in the 1980s. While dressing, she realised that her left arm could not hang normally against her left side, there seemed to be a bump on her left breast. When she took a closer look in the mirror, there appeared a bump, about the length of her half her finger: painful, but not excruciatingly so. Despite this, she still had to work and so when she arrived at the restaurant, she found a female member of staff and asked her to check for her in the restroom whether there was a bump or not on her left breast. The staff member confirmed it was so. The possibility of breast cancer loomed. My mother was not afraid of death but she was concerned about leaving behind six children and husband and so she did what she always did as a first port of call, she prayed.

Amazingly, over time, the lump disappeared, never to reappear again. It is of course, entirely possible that the lump was an enlarged lymphatic node or other non cancerous issues but whatever the medical problem, God responded to his daughter's cry for help. While this event can be dismissed as medically plausible, others cannot be so easily dismissed.

Upon arrival in the UK my mother had been under immense pressure. Financial worries, visa insecurities, lack of accommodation, the stresses and strains of looking after six children, a husband who was not then a believer and who was prone to gambling. Working without rest in a pressure-cooker environment began to tell and the lid eventually exploded.

One Sunday in 1972 her head felt very painful. She had just finished worship at church and was reluctant to go to hospital but her headache worsened. She felt as though flashing lights like that of an ambulance were twirling and screeching in her head. Knowing something was wrong, she asked my second brother, who was also at church, to take her to hospital. By the time they arrived at the Accident and Emergency of the Royal Infirmary, as it was then called, she was unable to move any part of her body, only her mouth. A friend from church had accompanied her and as she lay immobile on the hospital gurney, she asked her friend to pray for her; her head was in too much pain. At that moment, she heard a voice:

"Is your head painful? Wasn't Jesus' death on the cross for you even more painful?"

At that moment she realised just how much pressure she had been under since leaving Hong Kong: struggling and battling with work, children and husband. And with that realisation she fell unconscious.

On the day this happened, my father was in Edinburgh, visiting a friend. As he made a desperate dash back to Liverpool, the doctors gave the bad news to my second brother: She had ruptured capillaries in her brain and that there was little hope of recovery. The doctors even advised him to prepare for the inevitable and make funeral arrangements. My brother was devastated.

That evening when she woke she found herself in a ward. It was around that time that her pastor came to visit and asked if he could pray with her, the same pastor who had spoken to her about her mother and the illustration regarding the silver coins. She was more than eager and so, after going home to collect oil for prayer, he prayed over her, anointed her with the oil, then left. When she had fallen unconscious she had been unable to feel her legs or arms. Now, for four days she was not allowed to move as she lay on her back, with no pillow, and fed soup from a small cup. Nor was she given any medication. Doctors and nurses would come round, examine the chart hanging from the end of her bed and look confused. She appeared too well for a woman in her condition. By the fourth day, a Thursday, a consultant came to do his rounds. The consultant kept flipping the chart, looked at her, flipped the chart again and then huddled next to a window with the nursing sister and the junior doctors for a long discussion. He then walked back to look at her, returned to the huddled group and discussed some more. Finally, he returned to his prone patient and said four simple words: "You can go home."

It was an amazing moment. Without doubt, she knew God had healed her. To this day, there have been no lasting side-effects from an event that should have left her with severe disabilities, if not death. Friends and family were astonished. Even her own pastor who had prayed for her was surprised at how well she was when he visited her after her return home. The pressures she faced had not changed, but just as God had revealed to her his glory when she sought Him, now he had shown her his mercy. He had gifted her to us for a while longer.

Chapter 13

The Final Stretch Home

For the last twenty two years of her life, my mother lived in a small bungalow. Initially with my father and then, after his death, on her own. The transition from the previous large family home was, at first, difficult. The restaurant had been sold and there was conflict between my two eldest brothers but despite the loss of their life's work and unjust accusations from various parties, in this final stage of her life she also found satisfaction. Satisfaction because during this time, my father committed himself to God and my mother had again a church family that appreciated her spiritual gifts and was willing to nurture them. Most importantly, it was a time when she was finally able to allow God to fully heal the hurts and traumas she had suffered early in her life.

Oatmeal and Porridge

During his last few years my father suffered from diabetes and Parkinson's disease. As he deteriorated, my mother was his carer until he reached a stage when she was unable to look after him on her own and he was moved to a nearby nursing home, three minutes' walk away from their bungalow. Mum had partnered with my father on a full and eventful journey for over fifty years and although she knew he had committed himself into God's hands, when the time came for him to pass to his next adventure, she realised she was not ready.

On the day before Dad's death a close friend from church had been sitting with my mother at Dad's bedside. As evening approached, Mum suggested that her friend go home to get some rest, but her friend's response was that she was more concerned for my mother than my father. It was then that my mother realised she was not ready to let my father go; she could not let him go. With this sudden realisation, the two friends prayed. In my mother's words:

> "As soon as we finished, I knew; my heart was at peace. I knew that if I hadn't let go, my Heavenly Father would not force me."

With her heart at peace, she sat with him until 12am; she then returned home to cook some oatmeal. She had not been home long when my sister called her, urging her to return quickly. We felt Dad did not have long left. To our surprise, and indeed, some anxiety, her response was that we need not worry. She would finish her oatmeal porridge and then return. She did not tell us till afterwards, but as she sat by his bedside, she felt her Heavenly Father reassure her that her husband would not pass away till after dawn and that she should return home to strengthen herself with food and rest. We were less certain and upon our urging, she did return straight away, but sure enough, it was not until 6:30am that my father passed away, peacefully with his whole family around him and my mother, holding his hand. Even as she held his hand and reassured him that Jesus was coming to receive him, I could see she was filled with an inner joy. Together she urged us to sing worship songs over my father as he drew his final breaths. As she shared with us later:

> "My heart was so peaceful. There was no struggle or bitterness. My heart was instead full of thanks. Despite our difficult start I truly loved him. Why did I love him so much? Because I had been loved by God. I, who had been such a sinner myself."

Arrival of Spring

As a good friend of my mother pointed out, her name, Tung Lau, can also sound like winter lingers; (tung) winter (lau) lingers. It seems an appropriate way to describe her life; a life of persistent struggle against physical, emotional and spiritual difficulties, but all the while, in the hope and anticipation of the spring to come.

While her health permitted, she was still physically active in sharing the gospel with complete strangers that she would meet when out walking. Nearer home, she would take a proactive approach to the many naughty children who lived in her neighbourhood by inviting them inside. As one neighbour, now fully grown, recalls, 'Yer Choi Fa por por', or Cauliflower granny as they called her because of her shock of semi-permanently permed white hair, would sit them on the floor around her gas fire, hand out cups of tea and biscuits then share with them the good news of Jesus. All questions, however silly, were answered with complete seriousness and patience.

With my father's passing, she spent more time reminiscing the past but the relationship with her own mother still needed time to fully heal. Although she no longer hated her mother, she had dealt with that many years ago, she was still susceptible to bouts of self-pity and gut wrenching anguish at painful memories. But God is good. As the years progressed, such bouts of grief lessened and ironically, part of her emotional healing took place against a background of increased physical debilitation. The stubbornness that helped her through challenges and obstacles in life was also a character trait that resulted in relentless pain in her final years when, in a moment of obdurate stubbornness, she fell when she insisted on walking outside in icy weather. Discovered on a pavement near her home by a neighbour, she was rushed to hospital with a fractured hip and an emergency operation undertaken. A pin was put in place but the operation gave her problems for the remainder of her life; tendons and muscles were shortened during the hip replacement and she was to find it difficult to sit in one position for long periods. Coupled with severe arthritis, and her numerous other medical ailments, she would become increasingly immobile; using only her force of will and upper body strength to keep her walking a decreasing number of steps through the years. Yet despite her declining mobility, and increasing ailments, she came to find full peace in her tortured feelings towards her mother.

She knew of course that she was not the only one to have suffered at the hands of loved ones, but knowledge of another's pain cannot heal the pain in our own hearts. It took many years before she was finally able to speak of elements of the past without distress, but she was a woman who was acutely aware of her own sinfulness; a woman who always sought to see the good in others. I never heard her speak badly of my father, despite his many manifold faults; nor did I ever hear her speak negatively of any other person. Whenever I would broach negativity towards my father or anyone else, she would always find positives in them. Neither did she naively claim goodness for others. She, more than most, was aware of the hidden sins in our hearts. She was adept at reading people but the nearest she came to not speaking well of others would be to not speak at all. In effect, if she had nothing good to say, she said nothing.

When the time came for her to leave this life, the end came relatively quickly. She had been waiting in anticipation for a very long time, having been living in a great deal of pain for many years. She entered the A&E of the Royal Liverpool Hospital on the 8th of March and was admitted to a ward the next day with a lung infection. We, her family and friends, are grateful that covid restrictions were lifted enough to allow visitors to her bedside. My mother's pastor and his wife, who had left Liverpool the year previously, were, by God-directed coincidence, temporarily visiting Liverpool at the time. They were two of the visitors who saw her the evening before her death.

She was on oxygen and had little energy to speak or interact, but as I popped my head round the curtain to check if all was well, I was amazed to see my mother, propped up and radiant with joy. Her face was glowing. She had no fear, only yearning for the glory and beauty that had been revealed: previously in part, now to be revealed in full at last. She had entered the A&E on the 8th of March and, in the early hours of 10th March 2022 departed to her heavenly home. Spring had come at last.

Afterword

A Daughter's Journey

This short book has been many years in gestation. I had intended to write it when my father was still alive, and then, some years after his death, I made a stab at getting started. I knew my mother's stories were inspirational to many, myself included. I shared my intentions with her and received her blessing on the project. I interviewed her for details about her childhood and made notes but could never proceed very far when it came to setting down words to pages. It is only now, after her death, that I have been able to complete a journey that I began during her lifetime. And perhaps this is for the best.

There are many aspects of her life that she shared openly; her conversion, her struggles to stay honourable before God in a business environment; even her struggles with her illnesses but there is much that she felt unable to disclose easily to others. Her Near Death Experience and darkest days in the early years of her marriage were too personal and in the case of her Near Death Experience, too precious, to share gratuitously. Others, such as the betrayal of trust she felt from a Christian brother was too painful but also, she felt, unedifying to God. I have sought to keep the names of parties anonymous in this particular incident, but I feel that without its inclusion, we would be unable to fully appreciate, not only the difficulties she encountered, but also the sacrifices she made. The stories related in this short account are by no means exhaustive and my mother experienced pain and heartache from infighting amongst her own children and through her very long association with Christians and churches. Where else will we face the greatest pain if not from those we hold the most dear.

We are all fallible, very fallible; my mother included, but her faults were, in the main, a product of her own painful past. Her experiences of loss made her, by the standards of today, overly protective of her children and my father's extreme risk-disposed nature, meant that she had to become the counterbalance to his freewheeling schemes. One comical example took place soon after we had moved into Marlborough Road. Even though he could not ride and had no licence, my father bought a very large (in keeping with his general approach to life) motorcycle only to find a few weeks later his wife had dismantled it in fear that he would have an accident on the road and leave her children fatherless. To be fair to my father, once his shock had subsided his response became less of anger and more of amusement.

Thus it is that I have been able to share so much of my mother's life and of her life in Christ. She would not have wanted any honour in the telling, only that glory be given to God but as I set down her rich, eventful life's journey I was again struck by the simplicity and childlike nature of her faith. Whenever we encountered roadblocks in life and sought her advice, her favourite phrase was usually the same: "Look to God". So often, internally, I would roll my eyes and dismiss it as an oversimplification, a catch-all. How do we "look to God"? What are the steps, the specifics, did she not understand the minutiae of the problem at hand?

But of course, with time comes greater appreciation of immutable truths. For her, "Look to God" encompassed more than an unfocused gaze or a vague hope. It meant total reliance on His strength; a complete trust in His goodness and obedience to His commands, whatever the cost. She herself had experienced it to be true. So much of her life could have been consumed in the fires of hate, resentment, despair or aggressive pugnacity towards everyone around her. Instead, she allowed herself to be consumed by the love of God and I am forever grateful to my heavenly father that he gifted me with the love of an amazing mother. She had planned her own funeral twenty years in advance and a verse she wanted used sums up well a life fixed on faith, hope and love; the greatest of which is love:

> Because of the Lord's great love,
> We are not consumed,
> For his compassions never fail.
> They are new every morning.
> Great is Your faithfulness.

Lamentations 3:22-23

Mum and the author, soon after moving to
Narcissus House

Dad, hand pulling noodles

Mum, in chilly Liverpool, 1968

Exterior of restaurant at Marlborough Road

Acknowledgments

My thanks to all who supported me in prayer,
feedback and encouragement. Your friendships are
a joy to my soul.
Thank You.

About the Author

Annie is the youngest of six children. She was born in Hong Kong before arriving in England with her family when she was two years old. She has been a lawyer, journalist and theology student before, to her own surprise, becoming a primary school teacher in Hong Kong. Annie currently lives in the UK.

Printed in Great Britain
by Amazon

20595728R00079